OUR PLACE IN HISTORY
THE STORY OF WENDOVER

by Margaret Gosling

About the author

Margaret Gosling has lived in Wendover since 1975. For 22 years, between 1984 and 2006, she worked at Wendover C of E Middle School, and this, together with her active involvement in St Mary's Church has encouraged and supported detailed research into the surrounding area.

This enthusiasm, knowledge and deep love for the town has inspired Margaret to present popular and well-attended local history walks and presentations. Now retired, Margaret has been able to fulfil her long-held ambition to produce a comprehensive, chronological history of the development of Wendover and the lives of the people who have lived there.

First published in Great Britain in 2010 by Thinkography Limited.

Designed and typeset by Thinkography Limited. www.thinkography.com

Printed and bound by www.printondemand-worldwide.com

ISBN: 978-0-9566298-0-7

Contents

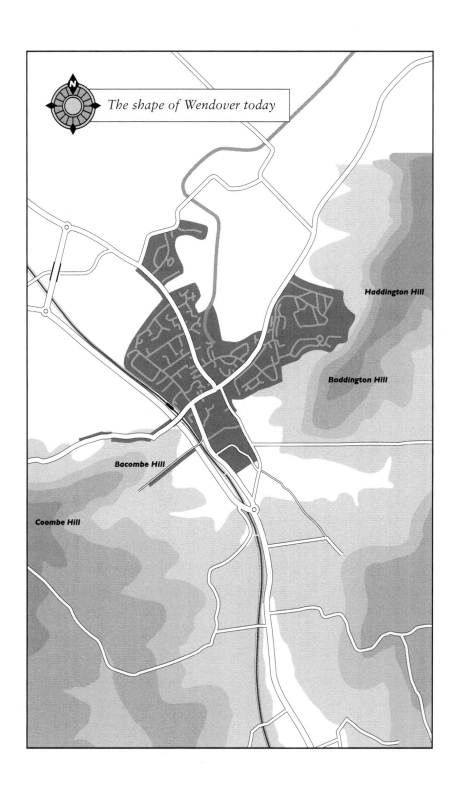

The shape of Wendover today

Haddington Hill

Boddington Hill

Bacombe Hill

Coombe Hill

Introduction

Situated in the south centre of Buckinghamshire, the picturesque town of Wendover occupies a position of impressive natural beauty, where the western escarpments of the richly wooded Chiltern Hills descend steeply into the fertile Vale of Aylesbury.

Standing on the Icknield Way, which is believed to be the oldest road in England, for it was a trade route in prehistoric days, Wendover is a place where the imprint of time goes very deep.

This book is a chronological account of Wendover's development into the place it is today. Because of its beautiful setting and its accessibility, Wendover has become a much favoured residential district and a popular touring centre for the Chiltern Hills.

There are already some wonderful books recording in detail the many aspects of its fascinating history. Having read this account, it is hoped that you will wish to explore the former publications for a deeper understanding of our place in history.

Margaret Gosling

1

The First Settlement

0 – 1000 AD

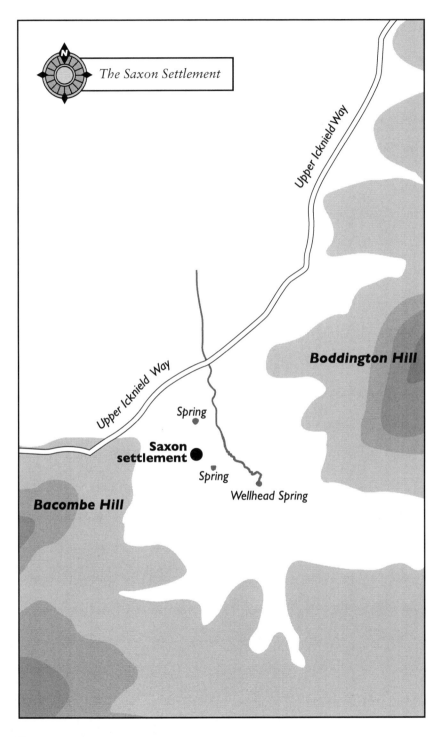

Wendover lies in the Chiltern Hills, at the head of the valley of the River Misbourne. The parish now covers almost 6,000 acres at 152 metres above sea level, flanked by Coombe Hill (257 metres), Bacombe Hill, Boddington Hill and Haddington Hill. At first, there were just the four hills here, all densely forested. From these hills emanated a number of natural springs. Crossing the area from east to west was an ancient trade route, now known as the Icknield Way.

Why would people choose to live here? Early people choosing somewhere to live permanently would need two important resources – good, fresh water to drink and wood with which to build dwellings and provide fuel for warmth and cooking food. Wendover had both in abundance. There were plenty of natural springs emerging from the wooded hills, the main ones arising on the edge of Witchell Meadow and at Hampden Pond, where they combine with the Wellhead Spring not far from St. Mary's Church.

Mr. E.J. Payne, who was a Wendover resident and high authority on the subject, believed that there was a settlement of considerable size at the foot of Bacombe Hill, close to the Icknield Way, in the early British Age. From Bacombe Hill there is a good view up and down this ancient route, essential to avoid attack by hostile tribes. Mr. Payne believed that as times became less turbulent, the Britons had abandoned their earlier settlement and descended to a lower and more sheltered situation. The first people to live here permanently were probably Celts. They lived a very simple life producing their own food, clothes and tools.

Britain was then invaded by peoples from Europe called Angles and Saxons. The Celtic people were pushed into Wales and Cornwall. The Saxon leaders were farmers who sought good land in river valleys on which to farm. Many local parishes along the Chiltern escarpment originated from Roman or Saxon farm estates, which gave them an agriculturally ideal mix of rich vale arable land, foothills pasture and high ground woodland, producing fodder for pigs and ample wood for building and fuel. The Saxons built their sturdy wooden houses in a circle within a wooden outer fence or stockade to keep out wolves from the forests. An aerial photograph of the area between Chapel Lane and Church Lane reveals a strange ring 60 metres in diameter, which historians suggest indicates the presence of an earthwork here. Christianity arrived in this part of England in about 700 A.D. The Saxons probably had a place of worship as part of their village. It would have been made of wood and be the only public building in the community.

There are several theories about the name Wendover. In Celtic times it may have been called *Gwaen-y-diffryn*, which means 'marsh in the glen'. The Welsh for 'white water' is *Gwynddwfr*, which, pronounced correctly, sounds like Wendover. In heavy storms, water gushing down the surrounding hills is white with chalk particles. In Saxon though, *wend* means 'winding stream' and *over* means 'bank' or 'shore'. Maybe this referred to the stream, which flowed from the Wellhead spring past the church northwards between the hills.

So, Wendover was probably settled by Britons, Celts and Romans but not until Saxon days do we find the first written evidence of a settlement in this area. Aelfheath was an Alderman of Hampshire and Wiltshire, but he owned land in Wendover. In his will of 970 A.D., he gave 'lands in Waendofron' to his kinsman, the great Eadgar, King of Mercians. From that time until 1564, Wendover belonged to the reigning English sovereign.

2

The Manor of Wendoure

1000 – 1200 AD

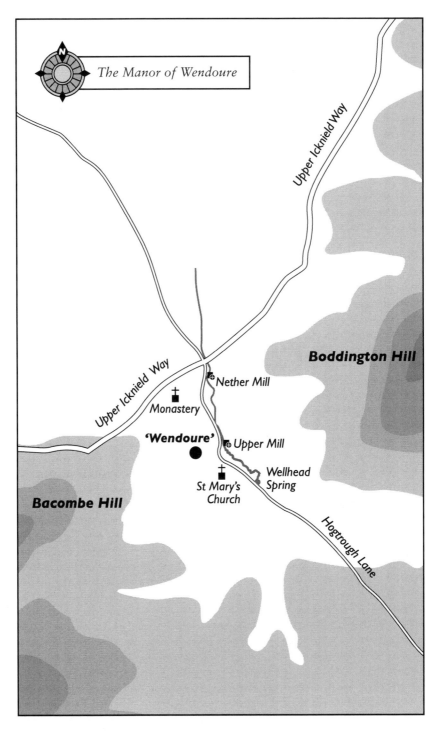

In those early times the Chiltern Hills were covered with woods and groves of beech so thick as to be almost impassable. These were home to wild beasts such as wolves, wild boar and wild bulls as well as robbers, outlaws and fugitives. So the villagers rarely strayed beyond their village. They worked hard growing their crops and tending their animals. They also kept pigs on the edges of the woodland.

The King's estate covered about 3,000 acres, half of which were used to grow crops. There were two watermills, which raised ten shillings per annum in taxes paid to the King to have grain milled. The natural spring at the Wellhead fed the mill pond, which is now the garden of Sluice Cottage. The Upper Mill stood just along from St. Mary's Church on the site of Heronpath House. When this 1970's house was built, the remains of a wooden watermill were found, Anglo-Saxon in origin. It was a breast mill, which receives the water at half of the height of the wheel. The spring water continued on its way to feed the Nether Mill, an overshot mill standing on the site of the Old Mill House, which now stands near the centre of the town.

There were two important routes for travellers close by. From the south and alongside the millstream ran the ancient green road called Hogtrough Lane, a reference to the practice by Saxon farmers of providing drinking water there for the swine kept in the woodland. This grassy track joined the Icknield Way, where the Clock Tower now stands, forming an important crossroads. The Icknield Way, which ran from East Anglia en route to the Thames River, crossing at Goring, continuing as the Ridgeway to Salisbury Plain, had been an important trade route since pre-historic times. Its route is now identified by the Tring Road and up Back Street to the Ellesborough Road.

The first Saxon chiefs had led the settlers to Britain and given them land. In return, the farmers worked for their lord. The land kept by the lord himself was called 'demesne' and Wendoure was a 'royal demesne' held by King Edward the Confessor from 1042 – 1066 A.D., who used it as a royal hunting ground. Hence, we have the names Kingswood and King's Ash up in the hills.

In 1066 A.D. the new king of England was Harold who fought and lost a great battle against William, Duke of Normandy, from France. William thus became King William I of England, known as William the Conqueror. The Normans divided the country into Manors and, as king, William now owned the Manor of Wendoure. In 1086 A.D. a very important document was created called the Domesday Book. William wanted to know exactly what he owned and its financial value. Wendover appears in the Domesday Book as Wendoure, a thriving community of 175 people. Unusually, there were no serfs listed here; the men were free to work for whom they wished. After the Conquest in 1066, Wendoure remained a royal manor for another 500 years, the sovereign usually bestowing it upon a member of his court. This person's title was Lord of the Manor.

People often ask why the parish church of Wendover is situated so far from the centre of the community. Christianity had been brought to this part of the country by St. Birinus in the 7th century and it is believed that a church made of wood was built at about that time by the Saxons. This was replaced by a simple Norman church, first in wood and then in stone, on the current site, which was where the settlement originated. Dedicated to St. Mary the Virgin it appears to have been attached to the Manor until rectorial rights were granted to the Priory of St. Mary Overy in Southwark in London, during the reign of Henry II (1154 – 1189 A.D.).

There is evidence to suggest that there was a monastery. This stood on the land now occupied by 'Time', 'Antiques at Wendover' and Bosworth House. Under the coach arch of these early 16th century buildings is a stone stoup or piscina set into the exposed flint and clunch wall. There is a deep cellar and rumours of a secret passage under the road across to the Manor Waste. When the footings of the new shops were dug, old timbers and brickwork were discovered underground, which may have been monastery kitchens. When Bosworth House was modernised in the 1920's some fine wallpaintings were discovered behind 17th century panelling. In the area on which the houses of Witchell were built, there were orchards and fishponds believed to be further evidence of a monastery nearby.

3

Market Forces

1201 – 1485 AD

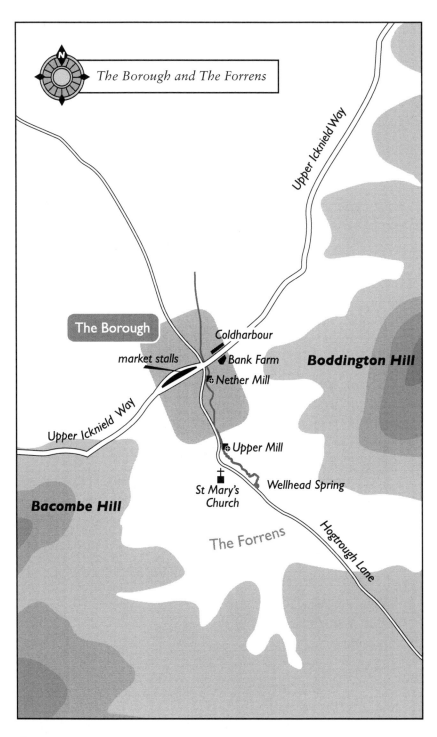

The Borough and The Forrens

Upper Icknield Way

The Borough

Coldharbour

market stalls

Bank Farm

Nether Mill

Boddington Hill

Upper Icknield Way

Upper Mill

St Mary's Church

Wellhead Spring

Bacombe Hill

The Forrens

Hogtrough Lane

The farming community by the church was extremely successful growing more crops than the inhabitants needed for themselves. There were no shops in those days and markets were the usual means of exchanging goods and services. In the early 1200's King John (1199 – 1216) granted to Hugh de Gurnay, the Lord of the Manor of Wendover, the right to hold a market once a week and an annual fair in June. Markets and fairs were usually held near the church in other places, but, in order to take advantage of the traffic along the Icknield Way, the farmers of Wendover set up their stalls along the route where travellers would pass and hopefully purchase their goods. The stalls were erected between what is now Back Street and the High Street. As trade increased, permanent buildings took their place. Gradually, during the early years of the 13th century, Wendover moved away from its original location near St. Mary's Church to these crossroads and thus became an important market town as well as a successful farming community. There were now two fairs in May and October.

The Manor was now divided into two parts. The Borough was the thirty acres inside the boundary now formed by Wharf Road to the north, Holly House to the east, the 'Shoulder of Mutton' to the west and Chapel Lane to the south. All buildings at that time consisted of timber cruck-framed structures filled in with wattle and daub. At The Old House, along Aylesbury Street, the original cottage's cruck roof is still visible in the north-facing gable end. In Tring Road, back in 1300, there existed a hospital of the Order of St. John. It comprised a three-sided barn, cold and uncomfortable. Hence, the name of Coldharbour, which survives today. Originally, it was for lepers, though one bed was separated and reserved for travellers. In time, as leprosy was eradicated, Coldharbour became a general hospital, maintained by charges on the villagers. The original farmhouse at Bank Farm is believed to be the oldest secular building still existing in Wendover. It was built in the early 1400's as an open hall. Three trusses and an arched tie-beam remain and may have been part of a large hall before present floors were added. In the area between Paradise House and the old watermill, there was at one time evidence of a convent called Paradise, which had exceptionally beautiful gardens, but this has long since disappeared. In Pound Street the cottages numbered 6 and 8 have 15th century crucks.

The Borough was administered by the Bailiff, the Constable and Dosoners who collected rents and taxes on behalf of the Lord of the Manor. This tiny community had the extraordinary right to send two burgesses to Parliament. In 1301 a Great Parliament was set up in Lincoln and Wendover sent two men, John de la Burg and Walter de la Hale, our first Members of Parliament.

The surrounding area of the parish was called Wendover Forrens or Fforence, just meaning 'foreign'. There were a number of farm houses and farm workers' cottages plus some grand residencies, mainly south of the Borough. These included The Hale and the Manor of Wivelsgate to the east, Bacombe Hill to the west, Wendover Dean, the Manor of Martyns and Mayertorne Manor to the south. The Hale farmhouse is where Sir Henry Colet was born in 1435. Fifteen years later he moved to London to train as a mercer's apprentice, becoming a wealthy dealer in expensive fabrics and twice Lord Mayor of London. Henry and his wife had twenty-two children of whom only one, John the eldest, survived to adulthood. Dr. John Colet, born in 1465, became the famous dean of St. Paul's Cathedral, friend of Erasmus and founder of St. Paul's School. Our secondary school in Wendover is named after John Colet.

The Forrens had the same set of officers as the Borough but they had no authority within the Borough and no right to a burgess. The two manors, Borough and Forrens, remained in the hands of the Lord of the Manor. In 1339, King Edward III granted Wendover to Sir John de Molyns. In 1371 it passed to Alice Ferrers, the King's favourite. Ten years later Richard II granted it to Thomas Holland (his half-brother) and in 1384 to his own wife, Queen Anne.

These commercial and administrative developments left the church isolated in the Forrens. Dedicated to St. Mary the Virgin it had been founded in or before the reign of Henry III in the 13th century by the Prior and Convent of St. Mary Overy in Southwark. We have a complete record of the vicars of Wendover from the time of Henry's reign. Records indicate that Christian worship took place here long before the present church building was begun during the first half of the 13th century. The earlier church was replaced by one built from clunch or chalk stone faced with flint from the Chiltern Hills. The walls of the chancel are probably the oldest part of the present church and the piscina let into the south wall is certainly one of the oldest features. The western part of the nave is the earliest part of the building, which can be dated by architectural details. Here the square columns, octagonal capitals and square bases are late 13th century in style, which coincides with the earliest recorded date of the church's existence, 1290. The eastern side of the nave and the tower date from the early part of the 14th century but their architectural details have been lost in later refurbishments. The chancel was widened, a vestry built north of the chancel and the south porch added during this period. A clerestory was added during the 15th century but the general exterior appearance has altered very little in the 500 years since. St. Mary's was of course a Roman Catholic church at that time. The congregation stood passively in the nave. The priest was separated from them by an elaborate rood screen and the Sanctus bell was rung to indicate the climax of the Mass.

The Borough Officers had no authority over the church because it stood outside the Borough. However, the two church wardens had the responsibility of making 'the Church Ale and their book of account'. The parishioners contributed malt to the church as a free offering in addition to their tithes. This was brewed by the church wardens or in some cases by the vicar, and on a stated festival, when the 'ale was fairly old', the parishioners repaired to the churchyard and there celebrated the wake or feast of the dedication of the church, even erecting booths. Each person paid a small sum called a 'scot' or 'shot' for the privilege of joining the festival. The proceeds usually went to the Rector rather than the Vicar.

These festivals became somewhat undignified occasions, with great excesses in eating, drinking and unseemly behaviour. After the Reformation they were totally banned.

4

Tudor Times

1485 – 1603 AD

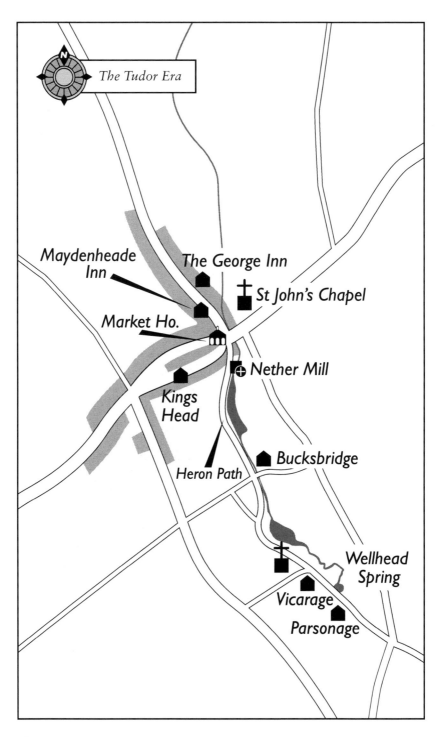

The Tudor Era

Maydenheade Inn

The George Inn

St John's Chapel

Market Ho.

Nether Mill

Kings Head

Heron Path

Bucksbridge

Wellhead Spring

Vicarage

Parsonage

The general layout of the centre of the town was established in Tudor times, community life now revolving around the crossroads on the Icknield Way. The population had grown to about five hundred people, mostly farm workers and their families. Hiring was usually conducted at the now twice-yearly fairs. The title farmworker covered a wide variety of skills and, as the community expanded and developed, other specialist trades and professions evolved. Travel was still difficult so most residents stayed in Wendover. Despite this, all able-bodied parishioners were charged four days wages per year to maintain the roads. In 1535 it was decided to raise the level of North Street *(now known as Aylesbury Road)* at its junction with Icknield Way due to flooding. The work was done by the poorest labourers just to give them paid employment. Under Elizabethan laws, Overseers of the Poor were responsible for looking after the poor of the parish, relief being given as bread, clothing or money.

The Borough began to look as it does now. Anything built before 1600 was likely to have a timber frame but these have mostly been disguised by later additions. Smaller houses had the first floor built out on projecting timbers called a jetty with the timber frame filled in with panels of plaster or brick. The road to the north, now known as Aylesbury Road, had several large houses and cottages along it. On the corner at the bottom of Back Street was 'The Maydenheade Inn' built about 1500. The cottages alongside, numbers 7, 9, 11 and 13, all have timber frames. The Old Cottage at No. 9 is the only one that remains as it was built with its jettied upper floor intact. The others have been underfilled with brick or flint. Numbers 19 to 21 date from the early 1600's and are also timber framed. The Old Manor Farmhouse is a 16th or early 17th century building and therefore timber framed as can be seen on the side wall. St. Anne's Close was built on what was the farmyard. Beyond here was a causeway across marshy land described in 1533 as 'very tedious and ill to pass by'. To the north of Wendover were damp meadowlands leading to the fertile clay lands of Aylesbury Vale. The long grass was cut in June and they became Lammas meadows, i.e. from 1st August, after the landowners' crops had been harvested, the villagers had grazing rights. The fields would be full of sheep and cattle put out to pasture.

The Old House was originally just a cottage with a cruck frame and Chiltern House has a 16th century rear wing. Sturrick House was built as an open hall, like Bank Farm. Dating from 1550 it also has a 17th century timber-framed rear wing and was once known as 'The Black Swan'. The other houses in this row are long and low, some with the remains of a jetty still to be seen and with handmade tiles covering the roofs. The original 'George Inn' near the corner of Tring Road was there in the 1500's serving the needs of the travellers on the Icknield Way.

The Tring Road was called East Streete. On the site of the Coldharbour, now occupied by Holly House was a chapel of ease. St. John's Chapel, connected to the Hospital of St. John, which stood there in the late 13th century, fell into disuse in Tudor times. The Coldharbour cottages were built as five houses and, as Lord of the Manor, belonged to Henry VIII. He settled the Manor on each of his wives in turn – Catherine of Aragon, Jane Seymour, Anne of Cleves and Catherine Howard. It is thought that it was also bestowed upon Anne Boleyn, whose father was 'Lord of the Towne of Ailesburie', and despite there being no written proof in her case, they have become known as 'Anne Boleyn's Cottages'. Behind the cottages was a vast, unhedged, open field rising up to grazing on the slopes of Boddington Hill. Beyond that was forest, through which ran the Icknield Way. To the south of East Streete stood Bank Farm with its original farmhouse built in the 1400's as a large open hall. Later, in the 16th century, proper chimneys were built and a floor added just above head height to make a two-storey dwelling, which still exists at the back. Where the Clock Tower now stands was an open field by the millstream and the Nether Mill, behind which was a 16th century barn, which later became Paradise House.

Returning to the crossroads and turning south, the first building on the left, the shop Number One was built in the early 1500's. As one can see from the side, it is a timber framed building with an underbuilt jetty infilled with brick and plaster. In 1577, Wendover had eight inns and one tavern. In addition to 'The Maydenheade' and 'The George' at the crossroads and close to the market there were 'The Swan', 'The Two Brewers', 'The King's Head' and 'The Shoulder of Mutton'. These all started life as inns in the 1500's. Near the top of the High Street, opposite the Manor Waste, stood a row of 16th century buildings built on what was believed to be the site of the monastery until the Dissolution of the Monasteries. Their basements were originally arched but are now filled in and behind were extensive orchards and several ponds. A few 15th century buildings have survived in Pound Street. Number 6 has three cruck trusses and Candle Cottage is a timber-framed building with two exposed cruck trusses.

The very early settlers had cleared many trees and shrubs and as the community increased, even more woodland was cleared. By 1620 there was less than half as much as there had been in 1086. Near the Borough there were small closes or fields bound by streams. These were divided into long, narrow strips for farming, very different from the large fields we have today. Bacombe Hill was a warren where rabbits and hares were bred for winter meat. Coombe Hill was unwooded grazing land. However, a large part of what is now the parish was still densely wooded. Bucksbridge is so called because deer came down from the woods to drink at the stream. There was a small house here made from wood and wattle-and-daub in the time of Queen Elizabeth the First, which was later enlarged to become Bucksbridge House. The two watermills survived until that time, the Nether Mill continuing production but the Upper Mill by the sluice was demolished about then and replaced by the Shift Mill to the north of the town. It is said that there was a heronry on the grounds beyond the millstream, near the sluice, where the herons came out and walked along the path, giving it the name Heron Path.

By the sixteenth century, St. Mary's Church was well established and previous to the Reformation held a position of much importance in the neighbourhood. In 1506, Lollards, the followers of John Wycliffe, were sent to make penance at the cross on the Rood Screen of Our Lady at St. Mary's Church. The living was in the gift of the Priory and Convent of St. Mary Overy, Southwark until the Dissolution of the Monasteries in 1539, when it passed to the Crown. In 1543, Henry VIII sold the Right of Patronage to the Bradshaw family, who in 1557 gave it to the Bishop of Lincoln, whence it passed to the Lord Chancellor in right of the Crown, and so remains. The full title of the incumbent of Wendover was Vicar of the Church of St. Mary's and Minister of the Chapel of St. John. This chapel, which stood on the Tring Road, came to be used by Dissenters at one time and later, when the Liturgy of the Church of England was introduced, the congregation far exceeded that attending the parish church. But, in 1550, the Bible in English was placed on a lectern in the nave of St. Mary's and St. John's Chapel was no longer used.

The Borough was now administered by an ecclesiastical organisation called the Vestry, their meetings taking place in the vestry north of the chancel of St. Mary's Church. The Vestry was formed by the Vicar, local farmers, tradesmen and landowners. They exercised wide powers, secular as well as ecclesiastical, electing the Churchwardens, Constables, Overseers of the Poor and Surveyors of the Highways.

In addition to the buildings of the time already described in this chapter, at the bottom of Back Street there was a two-storey building known at different times as Church House, Towne House or Market House. It was a rectangular timber and plaster structure, a half-timbered and gabled building standing on pillars above an open piazza, dating apparently from the latter part of the fifteenth century. What happened next is not clear but certainly at some time during the Tudor period, this became Wendover's first school. Thanks to careful records kept by the late Mr Ivor Pammenter, who was headmaster from 1965 until 1992, we know the following information about the early history of the school:

'For the real beginning of the school we must go back to the 16th century and the reign of Henry VIII. Somewhere about 1509, the year in which he founded St. Paul's School in London, John Colet sold a property known as Church House to the Churchwardens of Wendover for the sum of eight pounds.'

'In 1524 the lower part of the building was let off as shops while the upper storey was used as a school.'

'The Churchwardens, on behalf of the town, paid to John Colet £8 for a tenement called the Church House to be enjoyed by the Inhabitants, that some parts were divided into shoppes and letten to divers people and that the upper part was employed to teach Schollars till about 1613.'

'This revealed that about 1613 the inhabitants, having revived an ancient free market did cause the said Church House, otherwise called the Market House, otherwise the Town House, to be laid open and converted the lower part of the same into a market and extended the upper part for a Common School to teach children of the Parish of Wendover.'

The Market House

The site of the monastery

The stone stoup or piscina

The site of the Upper Mill

St Mary's Church

Bank Farm

Coldharbour Cottages

Cottages in Pound Street

The Red Lion, built 1619

5

A Bird's Eye View

1600 – 1700 AD

The Dame Mary Wolley map, 1620

Queen Elizabeth the First brought Wendover's royal connections to an end in the 1560's when she sold the Manor to William Hawtrey of Chequers. It was then inherited by his granddaughter, Dame Mary Wolley who, in 1620, commissioned the production of a very detailed map of the whole parish. This amazing document gives us a very good idea of what the parish was like in 1620. It shows each field and woodland with symbols to indicate the freeholders. All our modern routes are there but the main difference is the substantial network of minor tracks and access ways created to reach surrounding fields and villages. It measures 91 x 48 inches (231 x 122 cm) and consists of six pieces of vellum stitched together. This valuable map is the property of the current Lord of the Manor and is kept at the British Museum.

The Borough continued to expand and develop. Timber framing continued well into the 17th century but was beginning to be replaced by brick. The streets had different names from nowadays. Along the road 'to Alisbury' called North Streete, The Grange began as a much smaller house with the main entrance where the French windows are now. The Old House had a rear wing added and Chiltern House was enlarged. Its 300 year old staircase is still in use. Alongside 'The George' four cottages were built about 1635. In the Tring Road, then known as East Streete, the 17th century saw alterations to Coldharbour Cottages and the building of a large barn at Bank Farm. Paradise House, thought to be a 16th century barn originally, has a north wing dating from the 17th century. The house stands next door to the Nether Mill and was a malthouse and the home of the miller. Brook House was built on a timber frame beside the millstream in 1616.

Looking up the High Street many familiar buildings were now in situ. Next to Number One, The Forge Boutique and the shoe shop are timber-framed buildings of the 1600's and Woollerton House also dates from this time. 'The Red Lion' was built in 1619, making it one of the oldest public houses in Wendover. It contains oak panelling, fine old fireplaces and other interesting period features, but has been much restored and modernised.

In Tudor times, the Market House at the crossroads seems to have fallen into disuse and the lower part was divided into shops. In 1613 the local inhabitants had revived their ancient free market on Thursdays. They opened up the lower level as a market place again and two years later decided to enlarge it. This led to a dispute with the Bailiff of the Manor over a tax on market profits. The townsmen took their grievances to court in 1630 where it was ordered that the Towne House or Market House was the property of the town for charitable purposes. Therefore, the school on the upper floor was now owned by the town, supported by the Church, kept and paid for with the help of charitable bequests. In 1700, Sir Roger Hill gave £20 per annum for the education of twenty Wendover children. During the 17th century, a bell turret and a sundial were added and the northern bay was enclosed to form a cage or lockup, the stocks being placed near it.

Back Street lies on the main route of the ancient trackway, which ran down the Tring Road, through the town, continuing along the Ellesborough Road. This was originally the main street and a number of 17th century cottages lined its route, but, as the town developed, Back Street became a minor road running parallel to the High Street. The most imposing building in Back Street is Vine Tree House. It was the farmhouse of Vine Tree Farm, which extended behind as far as Perry Street. Its 16th or 17th century timber framing is exposed on the eastern flank and shows how the timber frame of a larger house was constructed.

Dobbins Lane was known as Dame Agnes Lane, a narrow track leading to farmland. Pound Street was known as West Streete. Many of its pretty row of cottages were built in the 17th century; number 5 and numbers 9 – 23 were all built then, some with thatched roofs while others were tiled. At the top stood 'The Shoulder of Mutton'

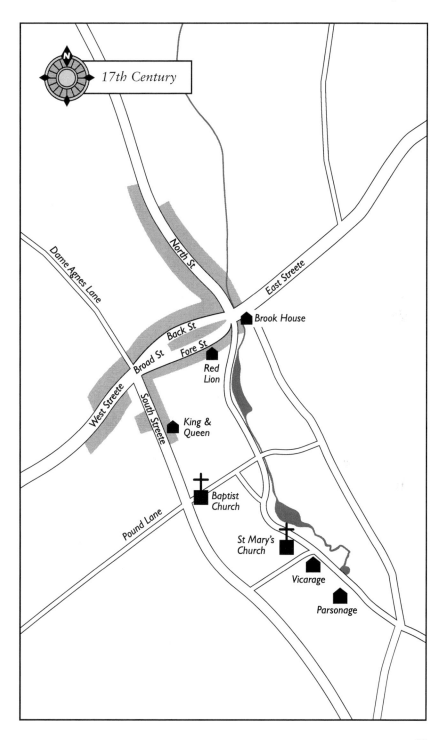

and the house next to it both built using wattle-and-daub. 'The King and Queen' in South Streete is part 17th century with a timber frame but with later extensions. Opposite 'The King and Queen' there are some timber-framed cottages with tiled roofs. Their jetties have been underfilled with bricks. Numbers 40, 42, 28, 24 and 24a were all built in the 17th century. The tiny cottage at number 28 dates from 1620 and is now Grade II listed. This wattle-and-daub construction has been totally restored in keeping with the original by the present owner. The pound for the detention of straying livestock was just beyond 'The King and Queen', hence the name Pound Lane on the map. It was later removed to West Streete, which then became known as Pound Street. Further down South Streete, Baptists began to meet in two cottages until 1649, when their purpose-built chapel was erected on land donated to them by John Baldwin, then Lord of the Manor.

Our MP in 1623 was John Hampden, who was a Buckinghamshire squire with a family estate at Great Hampden. In 1621, with help from his solicitor William Hakewill who lived at Bucksbridge House, he restored parliamentary rights for Wendover. In 1623, at his own expense, he became MP for Wendover and fiercely opposed both James I and Charles I. In 1636 he became a national figure by his refusal to pay ship money levied on his land, a tax invented to pay for protection of the South Coast. Charles' attempt to have Hampden arrested led to the outbreak of the Civil War in 1642. John Hampden died on 24th June 1643 at Thame from wounds sustained in the fighting. There is a statue of him in Aylesbury's Market Square and our infant school is named after him. He was never our Lord of the Manor but his descendants were. In 1660 his son Richard purchased the Manor and also became our MP. William Hakewill died aged 81 in 1655 and was buried in the chancel of the church.

The church was at a low point in the early 1600's. By 1637 the vast majority of country churches were in a poor condition. Religious disaffection was a major factor in the opposition to James and Charles, not least in Buckinghamshire. The people of Wendover were largely sympathetic to the Parliamentary cause and in 1642 Oliver Cromwell spent a night at 'The Red Lion'. In August of that year, Parliamentary troops passing through Wendover burnt the altar rails in the church. Other buildings also suffered as a result of the Civil War. Oxford was sympathetic to the King and this led to skirmishes along the Chiltern border lands. In 1643, Prince Rupert and his soldiers passed through Wendover. In March that year Mrs. Armitage, the wife of the Vicar of Wendover, baked some apple pies for the Royalist troops but, before they could eat them, they were called away and the pies were eaten by Parliamentary soldiers instead. Cromwell's men suspected the Reverend Armitage of having Royalist sympathies and he was turned out of the living that he had held for nearly thirty years.

On Dame Wolley's map, to the south of St. Mary's Church are marked the Parsonage and the Vicarage. The Priory of Southwark was originally the owner of the church and the lands attached to it so when their representative was resident in Wendover, he would use the Parsonage. All spiritual duties were conducted by the vicar who resided at the Vicarage. The entrance to the church was then from this side through the south porch. The Parish Registers for Baptisms were started in 1626. In 1665, the Great Plague struck the parish. Morgan Godwin, the Vicar at the time, recorded that 'seventy-three people had died of distemper and were buried' but their names were never recorded as registers for marriages and burials only started in 1670. In his well respected work on the history of Wendover, Sir Leonard West quoted the Parish Register of Marriages between the years 1678 and 1686, when among the bridegrooms' occupations were hemp dressing, weaving, cloth working, lace making, collar making and chair making. Several of the church bells were dated in the 1600's. Bells were originally installed to call the faithful to prayer and were rung erratically but, in about 1650, efforts were made to introduce a set of rules for ringing which are followed to this day.

6

The Changing Face of Wendover

1700 – 1836 AD

The appearance of the town changed considerably during the 18th century. Smart new Georgian frontages in red brick or plaster were added to the substantial timber structures from earlier periods. In addition many new buildings were constructed in the Georgian style. Together they stamped the character of Georgian architecture on so much of the town centre.

The 'Maydenheade Inn', which had stood on the corner of Back Street and North Street since 1500, was demolished to make way for the 'Junction Inn', an important overnight stop for stage coaches between Banbury and London. One can still see where the coaching arch was before being bricked up. The cottages on that side, with the exception of Number 9, had their jetties filled in with brick or flint. Numbers 15 and 19 were newly built in brick in the late 1700's, while numbers 21, 23 and 25 were updated at this time. The Manor Farmhouse was also given a façade and beyond its farmyard stood a newly built home. The Grange was given a brick façade with the addition of a Doric porch. Its flint wall also dates from this time. In 1768 there were cottages between the Manor Farmhouse and the Grange, which survived into the 20th century. The Old House was given a fine façade and new roof tiles in 1789. It is joined by a large square carriage arch to the cottages next door where Georgian frontages were added to numbers 32 and 34a and to Chiltern House in 1725. Numbers 26 and 24, known as Archway Cottage, date from the 18th century as does the main part of The Red House. Number 18, Lime Cottage has a brick façade on an older structure while number 16, Brook Cottage, was built in Georgian times. Numbers 10 to 14 gained a frontage on an older building and 'The George' was rebuilt at this time.

Along the Tring Road, Rose Cottage at number 5 was updated in the 1700's and in 1769 'The Packhorse' inn was built at the top end of Coldharbour Cottages. A whole new building was added to the front of Bank Farm but the old mediaeval structure survives at the rear. In 1768 a windmill was built but later removed. Hale Road at this time was called Paradise Lane or Chesham Road. Hazeldene Cottage was a newly built Georgian house, Paradise House gained a new frontage and Brook House had a stucco front added in the late 18th century. The Old Mill House was newly weather boarded.

The High Street was called Fore Street, where it ran parallel to Back Street and then opened out to an area called Broad Street. The buildings to the left, numbers 1, 3 and 5 were re-fronted with brick and numbers 11 and 13 newly built in local, handmade bricks. The Market House seems to have been untouched by this wave of modernisation. A writer of about 1800 described its appearance as 'particularly mean' and another speaks of 'the unsightly market house built of timber and plaster in the style of Henry VIII's time'. There was still a market in the market place on Thursdays and the people of Wendover kept and paid for the school in the upper storey until 1838. Beyond this new buildings appeared at numbers 14 and 16, and numbers 20, 22, 30 and 32 were all given new frontages. Beyond Bosworth House on the left the premises by Floyds Yard started life as two houses. Numbers 29 and 33 were also new at this time.

Along South Street the brick cottages with slate roofs date from the 1700's. The pound having been removed from outside 'The King and Queen' to West Street, this became known as Pound Street, its purpose being to house livestock overnight on their way to market. Number 7 Pound Street was a new cottage while numbers 21 and 23 were given a new brick frontage as were 10 and 12 on the opposite side. 'The Shoulder of Mutton' now had a Georgian brick facing. In Back Street, Summer Cottage and Autumn Cottage were brand new.

At the beginning of the 18th century the Borough was still predominantly farms and there were barns where Budgens supermarket stands now. Vine Tree Farmhouse in Back Street was updated with a brick façade and Lime Tree House was built as an 18th century farmhouse serving a farm to the rear. Most people were farm workers as had always been the case. Some were in occupations related to the farming industry. The most important man in any farming community was the blacksmith who shod the horses, made and repaired implements and tools, supplied the wheelwright with iron parts for his vehicles and made nails, hooks, latches, hinges, fire irons, chains, well fittings and parts for the church clock. In 1741 there were three blacksmiths but by 1798 there were nine.

However, many businesses started during this period and in 1718 the first fire engine was installed, paid for by local business people. By 1800 there were a chandler, six bakers, five butchers, three barbers, an apothecary and three drapers who sold fabrics and sewing requisites. There was a busy tailoring and dressmaking industry and shoes were made here. In Tring Road there was a tannery. A malting and brewing industry was established behind 'The King's Head'. There were several maltsters including the Franklin family. Four coopers, all from the Caudrey family, made barrels to transport Wendover ales to neighbouring towns.

There were also changes in the Forrens. The roads were improved considerably in this century by the setting up of Turnpike Trusts. The Wendover to Buckingham Trust was created in 1721 and levied tolls from just north of The Grange to Walton in Aylesbury. The money raised was used to maintain the roads. In 1763 a 16th century building to the north of the town was refurbished and opened as an inn called 'The Marquis of Granby'. It advertised its 'stables and pasture and good accommodation for drovers and their cattle'. The tall pine trees on the other side of the road were used as a landmark to guide drovers to suitable overnight stopping places. Until 1794 the fields looked much as they did in Tudor times. Many of the names of these fields are still in use today. Worlds End, Upper Ashbrook, Haglis, Reddings, Bryants Acre, Pennings and Honey Dean have survived. Then the Government introduced a law called the Enclosures Act to improve the efficiency of food production for a growing population. A private Act of Parliament was passed to enclose the open fields of the parish of Wendover. The old, narrow fields disappeared and larger fields enclosed by hedges were created changing the landscape dramatically. The cottagers were no longer able to collect food from the wild without risking arrest for poaching.

More change was wrought by the building of the Wendover Arm of the Grand Junction Canal. An Act of Parliament was passed in 1794 to build the canal as a reliable feeder of water to the main canal. It followed the line of the existing millstream tapping the succession of the many natural springs from the Wellhead through to the area of Wharf Road. The original access to the head of the new canal was from the end of Clay Lane but in 1796 local magistrates agreed to the closure of this route and Wharf Road was built purely to gain access to the canal and ended at the wharf. Beyond was Manor Farm and a great barn standing where the John Colet School stands now. Hampden Pond was created at this time and in 1797 the Halton or Weston Turville Reservoir was built. Between here and Wharf Road there was farmland and water meadows. When the Upper Mill at Bucksbridge was closed, Shift Mill had been built here but the millstream dried up after the Wendover Arm was built and Shift Mill ceased production. Mill Cottage still stands at the end of Castle Park Road. Completed in 1797 the canal was used to convey hay and straw from Wendover for the draught horses in London and to bring back manure for use on the fields. Coal, timber, other heavy goods and occasionally cattle for market were also transported.

In 1795 the site of the windmill was open fields bounded by the Aylesbury Road and on the south side by a track known as Townsend Close, later to become a footpath to Dobbins Lane. Across the Aylesbury Road another track led to the construction site of the new canal. The windmill was built between 1796 and 1804 by John Phillips of Vine Tree Farm. It was a grist mill of octagonal brick construction standing 66 feet high with walls three feet thick. It required 500 tons of bricks brought by donkey from Cholesbury. The cap is eighteen feet in diameter and is reputedly the largest in England.

The Aylesbury Road has been known in the past as Castle Road and Castle Ditch. Castle House, a neat square villa was built there about 1800 and has been known at different times as The Castle, Castle

The canal wharf then and now

The windmill, completed in 1804

House, Castle Villa, Cavendish Villa and Cavendish House. Richard Chandler was the MP for Wendover from 1761 until 1768. He married a member of the family of the Dukes of Devonshire and took their family name of Cavendish.

In 1700 the Manor was held by the Hampden family. However, much of the property was owned by the Verney family and many families lived in properties owned by Earl Verney. His tenants lived rent-free on the understanding that, in the event of an election, they would all vote for their landlord's chosen candidate. In 1768 a local lacemaker, Mr. Atkins, brought in a surprise candidate, Sir Robert Darling, who won the election. The Earl promptly dispossessed his rebellious tenants banishing them from the Borough. They housed themselves in a motley collection of shacks and tents known as Casualty Meadow. This was beyond the Borough boundary on land where the Manor Road Estate is now. When three rows of ten terraced cottages were built along the Tring Road they were known for many years as 'Casualty Row'. Alternative names were Thirty Houses and York Buildings. Wendover was at the time one of the most corrupt constituencies in the country. Earl Verney's attempt to become an MP himself in 1784 was again thwarted by the electors who, at a secret meeting, received £6,000 to be distributed among them.

The first Congregational Chapel was built in the Tring Road in 1811. In South Street local Baptists had been meeting since the 1640's in two cottages but in 1735 a purpose-built chapel was erected, rebuilt in 1770 and enlarged in 1833. Bucksbridge House became the grand house it is today when a new Regency style front was added.

The population of Wendover remained static for many years but, by the first national census in 1801, numbers had risen to 1,397. Virtually all local government functions were still carried out by the Vestry led by the Vicar. In 1799 this was the Reverend Joseph Smith, who set up the very first Penny Savings Bank in St. Mary's Church, in the vestry north of the chancel. The Vestry's responsibilities included law and order, highways and parish relief. Until 1792, there were six poorhouses on the south side of West Street (Pound Street), where the railway cutting is now. In 1794, a mile south of the town, where the Jet Garage stands now, stood Tenhouses, a row of cottages for the poor of Wendover, but in 1834 the Poor Law took away any local responsibility for their poor and they were sent to the workhouse five miles away at Bledlow.

The Georgian frontage of Vine Tree Farm House in Back Street

The Regency frontage of Bucksbridge House

The Old Mill House
(Nether Mill)

The windmill as a
residence today

Casualty Row, later known as York Buildings

7

Crossroads

1837 – 1901 AD

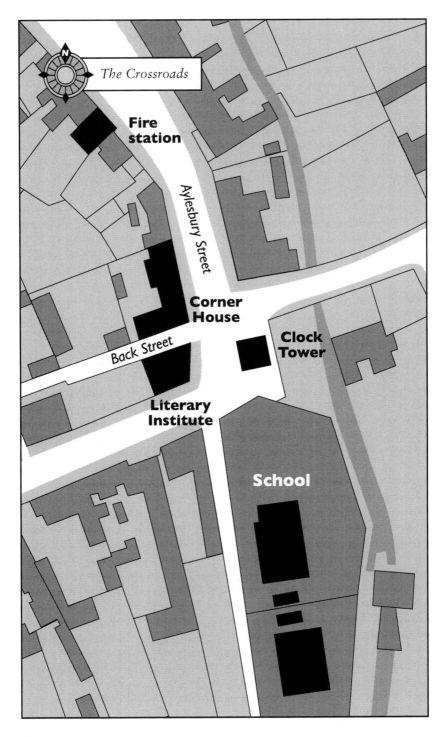

The Manor of Wendover had come into the hands of the Smith family when, in 1795, it was bought by Robert Smith, a leading banker and the first Lord Carrington. Soon afterwards he conveyed it to his brother Samuel Smith (1745 – 1834), who lived at Woodhall Park in Hertfordshire. As in mediaeval times, much of the land and buildings in the Borough belonged to the Lord of the Manor, who in 1837 was Abel Smith (1788 – 1859), son of Samuel. After a great deal of building activity in Georgian times, the appearance of most of the town stayed much the same until 1900, but, due to the generosity of the Smith family, major changes took place at the crossroads.

In 1838 the charity school was still housed in the Towne House above the market place. This building was now at least three hundred years old and Abel Smith decided that it should be taken down. Next to the Towne House, on the corner of Back Street and Aylesbury Street stood an old coaching inn, now used for parish affairs and also owned by the Lord of the Manor, who lent it, rent free, for use as the school. Lessons were taught on the upper floor, boys and girls in separate classes and outside was a small garden and playground. It was also the headmaster's house. In 1840 the school became a National School supported by grants from the National Society, the Church of England's society for promoting church schools and became known as St. Mary's National School. For the first time in three hundred years, it received regular financial help from outside the parish. Very few records of the school exist from the period 1838 – 1867 but we know that by 1862 there were about fifty pupils, the youngest of whom were eight years old. On the ground floor were the Parish Rooms in which divine service was held on Sunday and Wednesday, and lectures once a week. Twice a year the Lord of the Manor used the room to collect his rents.

In 1842 Abel Smith provided the main part of the Clock Tower as a small market hall and lockup to replace the old Towne House across the street. It was twenty-one feet square with a short brick tower topped by a turret and weathervane. The lower part of the building was enclosed by iron gates and the market was held there every Tuesday. The actual clock was added in 1843 at a cost of £90, raised by 'contributions from the Vicar, Churchwardens and Occupiers'.

From 1837 until 1850, Wendover had a young and energetic evangelical vicar appointed to his first ministry. The new vicar, the Reverend Spencer Thornton, who was a nephew of Abel Smith, found St. Mary's Church in an appalling state and many social problems in the town. In 1840, Lipscomb's report on Wendover stated that there were too many public houses and that the market consisted of 'a meagre assemblage of peasantry from contiguous districts standing at the corners of the streets with baskets of straw plait, and at the doors of the public houses'. Drunkenness was a serious problem both nationally and locally. The Reverend Spencer Thornton became a most zealous parish priest known as 'the Boy Missionary'. He stopped Sunday trading, promoted Sunday closing of public houses and formed the Wendover branch of the Church of England Total Abstinence Society. He organised weekly savings by the poor, which were returned to them during the winter months in food, clothing and fuel. The houses were heated by coal fires and coal was needed for cooking, so in 1841 he set up the Coal Club, bringing coal from the pits in Derbyshire and Staffordshire by canal to Wendover. He was pivotal in the foundation of St. Mary's National School for the poorer children of the parish. A library of 150 religious books was created, the subscription for its use being one penny per month and a wheelchair was provided to convey infirm people to lectures in the parish rooms and to church. As well as being a great leader of social reform in the town and closely supervising the running of the school, he found time to have the church 'painted and beautified'. Sadly, he died suddenly at the age of thirtysix, in a street near King's Cross Station in London.

Despite the building of the new market hall, by 1847 the Tuesday market was in decline and no longer warranted a purpose-built market place. The parish fire engine, a hand-pumped, horse-drawn

Corner House

The Literary Institute and Clock Tower

vehicle, was housed in a small, shed-like building at the foot of the High Street. In 1870 it was decided to move the fire engine into the Clock Tower, where there was ample room for its equipment. Philip Smith, the third son of Abel Smith, was now Lord of the Manor and he was responsible for the rebuilding of the Clock Tower. Horizontal slots with heavy cast-iron linings were cut into the supporting piers to accommodate the wheel hubs of the fire engine. The upper part of the tower was increased by another ten feet and capped by a small timber belfry and spirelet, the bell being used to summon the men of the fire brigade. A new drinking fountain and a horse trough were added 'providing refreshment for man and beast'.

However, seven years later, the fire engine was moved from the Clock Tower to a small building on the west side of Aylesbury Street, where it remained until the 1960's. The old stocks and lockup or cage were moved to the Manor Waste where the War Memorial now stands, known as Cage Bank. But, at the focal point of the three main streets, the Clock Tower has become the symbol of Wendover.

When the old Towne House was demolished the vacant site was used to build the Literary Institute. It was built in 1863 by Philip Smith as a memorial to his father Abel who had died in 1859. It provided facilities for several generations of Wendover's citizens with commodious reading rooms, a library of books for circulation and meeting rooms for local societies.

The old coaching inn loaned by the Lord of the Manor back in 1838, was no longer suitable as a school. By 1869 there were eighty-nine boys and seventy girls on roll plus a night school and a parochial lending library in the house. Between the millstream and the Heron Path, to the south of the Clock Tower, was land owned by the Lord of the Manor. It was occupied by a ropemaker called Charles Featherstonehaugh and known as Featherstone's Rope Walk. He made 'bell ropes, halters, scaffold cords, clothes lines, rick cloths and every kind of string', but in 1869 he moved to new premises further down the Heron Path by Bucksbridge to make way for a new school. The Lord of the Manor, Philip Smith, gave to the vicar, his brother the

Reverend Albert Smith, and the Churchwardens 'all that piece of land containing three roods and seventeen perches or thereabouts called the Rope Walk... for a school for the education of children and adults or children only of the labouring, manufacturing and other poorer classes in the Parish of Wendover'. A brand new school, designed by G.E. Street and built by the local firm of Holland and Senior, opened on the 7th December 1869. Philip Smith had employed an Oxford architect, William Wilkinson, to design the Literary Institute and the rebuilding of the Clock Tower, in the fashionable Gothic style of mid-Victorian architecture. Along with the new school building, the whole area was conceived as an integrated design intended to enhance the centre of the town.

Next door to the mill, the new school was a great improvement on the cramped conditions of the old inn. Mr. Arthur G. Fleming was the schoolmaster and Miss Sarah A. Holden, the schoolmistress, and boys and girls were taught separately. The children wrote on slates and there were lessons in reading, writing, arithmetic, history, geography, music and singing, drawing and drill (PE). The girls also learned needlework. There was a great deal of learning of poetry to recite from memory and the Catechism was taught as well as hymns. The Vicar, the Reverend Albert Smith, and the curate, Mr. Willis, came in regularly to teach scripture and there were visits to St. Mary's Church on feast days and saints' days. The children were keen to learn but it was not made easy for them. The older children were often absent, haymaking, potato picking, strawplaiting or 'minding the baby' and there was a lot of illness, including epidemics of measles, whooping cough or scarlet fever. Parents had to pay the school in those days and some children were absent because their parents had no money.

In 1876, boys and girls were taught in the same class for the first time and in 1879, a new wing was built, at the expense of the Reverend Albert Smith, alongside the mixed school as a new school for the infant department. There were several changes of schoolmaster but the best known was Mr. John George Bushell from 1883 – 1907, a hard master at times but a much respected and thoroughly good teacher.

The schoolmaster was supported in the running of the school by the Managers, just as we have Governors now. The school was an integral part of community life, being at the heart of the town geographically, and closely linked to the farming year. The summer holiday was called the Harvest Holiday and often did not start until the very end of July or even August, when the harvest was ready for reaping. There were extra days off school for Sunday School treats and other local events.

8

The Victorian Era

1837 – 1901 AD

The Victorian Era

When Victoria became the queen of this country in 1837, Wendover was still very much a farming community. Most adults worked on the farms or had jobs associated with farming and, as there was no law that made children go to school, many of the children worked on the farms as well. Horses were the main means of transport and were important to the farmers for work in the fields. The population having risen by about forty per cent between 1800 and 1830, it remained static after that and was about two thousand in 1900.

The populated area of the town, the Borough, remained compact being Aylesbury Street as far as Wharf Road, Tring Road up to Clay Lane, the High Street and Back Street, South Street as far as Witchell and Pound Street. Many houses were small farm houses with wide stable doors through which the animals could pass to the farmyard beyond. There were gardens and paddocks near the houses, which enabled the farmers to house the livestock instead of on common lands such as The Clay and Malm Fields that extended towards Boddington Hill. The majority lived in small cottages heated by coal fires on which they also cooked. The roads were only roughly made and became very muddy in wet weather. In winter snow made everyday life even more difficult, so people lived, worked and shopped in Wendover.

Throughout the Victorian era the sounds and smells of the farmyard were still an integral part of life in the town. In 1837 there were twenty-five farms in the parish as a whole, ten of which had farmyards within the Borough. Twice a year, on 13th May and the 2nd October, large agricultural fairs were held where farmers exchanged livestock and supplies and employed labourers. One resident, Harry Floyd, recalled 'I can remember when the High Street seemed to me to be full of sheep, calves, horses, ponies, etc., with vociferous men trying to bargain with each other, and I have seen as many as a hundred traps and horses in the yard of 'The Red Lion' on fair day'. At the end of the century the May Fair was still the annual Cattle Fair when Pound Street was full of pens of sheep and the London Road was packed with cattle. The public houses did a roaring trade with the drovers and cattle men. The October Fair gradually became a pleasure fair only.

In 1851 there was a national census, a copy of which is available in Wendover's public library. This records where people lived and their occupations. For instance, in the High Street as well as farmers there were a butcher, a tailor, a tea dealer, cabinet maker, master bricklayer and several innkeepers. The farms in the centre were beginning to disappear and by the end of the century had given way to supporting trades. As farming gradually gave way to industry and commerce, the High Street became a very lively place. There were good shops and people did not go elsewhere to do their shopping for there was no transport. There were butchers, bakers and grocers and a department store called Freeman's. In between there were still blacksmiths and harness makers.

The first row of buildings on the left had their shop fronts added during the nineteenth century. Number One was a butcher's shop, The Forge Boutique was a harness maker's shop selling a wide range of leather goods and behind stood a blacksmith's forge and a farmyard with large oak-beamed barns and stables. 'The Red Lion' was the centre of social life in Wendover for many years. The road from Aylesbury brought travellers by stagecoach from Banbury. The passengers stayed overnight in the many inns here including 'The Red Lion'. From 1830 onwards a daily stage coach set off from 'The Red Lion' each morning arriving at 'The Bull Inn', Holborn, five hours later and returning each evening. In 1875, Robert Louis Stevenson, whilst on a walking tour, spent an evening at 'The Red Lion' and wrote in glowing terms about the comforts of its parlour. The farm behind the inn was used for agricultural events such as ploughing matches. In 1900 a drastic restoration took place giving it its handsome timbered exterior. Beyond 'The Red Lion' extra houses were built about 1865, which have been used for many different shops and businesses since.

Next to Hogarth House was a walled orchard and 'The King's Head' behind which was a brewery. There had been a malting and brewing industry since the 17th century but the Wendover Brewing and Malting Company was established in 1824. The Caudrey family of coopers made the barrels to export the local beer to neighbouring towns and carts laden with barrels of beer were a common sight up and down the High Street. In 1900 there was a fire behind the brewery, which was successfully extinguished by the fire brigade, using the old manual fire engine to pump water from the lower Witchell pond.

Next to 'The King's Head', in the 1890's, stood a double-fronted shop run by Mr. Edwin King and his daughters. It was a farm outfitters, selling overalls, wellies, children's clothes and long woollen underwear. Across a carriage arch stood a farmhouse with a farmyard behind and then an old blacksmith's forge, run for generations by the Carter family. When this became vacant in 1888 Joseph Floyd, a wheelwright and coachbuilder set up his business there. Next door was another harness maker's shop. The wheelwright and harness maker were kept busy for farmers would come from the surrounding district bringing their carts, wagons and harnesses for repair.

On the opposite side of the High Street, between the Literary Institute and Great Lane, there was a variety of shops, including Pearce Brothers Stores, which sold a wide range of goods from flour to methylated spirits. Above Great Lane, where they had stood for two hundred years, were 'The Swan' and 'The Two Brewers'. Behind, in Back Street, stood the village pump, the only source of water for drinking, cooking and washing for most people before the advent of mains plumbing. Here, the local people came to fill their buckets and exchange a little idle gossip while waiting their turn. Chandos Court was home to lace makers, straw plaiters, a shoe maker and a chair maker and the Deering family ran a laundry. Vine Tree Farm survived as a working farm into the twentieth century. Between Vine Tree Farmhouse and the top of Back Street were a number of cottages. The garden of Pear Tree Cottage was where The Chocolaterie now stands.

The wider open area at the top of the High Street known as Broad Street, or the Manor Waste, could be used by anyone. It was the property of the Lord of the Manor but was used by farmers driving their animals to market and for the twice-yearly agricultural fairs. From 1868 onwards there were gas street lamps, which had to be lit and extinguished each night by the lamp lighter. Overlooking the Manor Waste was Wendover's department store. Frederick Freeman started his business as a chemist and druggist in 1855. By the end of the century, with the help of his family, it had expanded to include a ladies' and gentlemen's outfitters, a tailor's, a milliner's, draper's, bookseller and stationer's. Herbert Freeman was a photographer and he set up Chiltern Studios in the shop. The first post office in Wendover started at Mr. George Brackley's shop in the lower part of the High Street but later moved to Freeman's with Mr. Freeman as Postmaster until 1915.

At the corner of Dobbins Lane and Pound Street stood another grocer's shop and next door a bakery, established in the 1830's by William Thompson and run by the family well into the 20th century. Number 21 Pound Street was a butcher's shop run by the Goodson family with a slaughterhouse at the end of that row. On the corner of Pound Street and South Street there was a confectioner's shop and printing premises. The Wendover Hall was built in 1860, becoming the Mission Hall of the Buckinghamshire Evangelistic Mission in 1880. Opposite stood Albert Payne's rope and sack business. Originally at Rope Walk by the Nether Mill, the business had moved after the new school was built in 1869, and the ropes were made between the millstream and Hampden Meadow.

The millstream was much wider then between the Nether Mill and the 'Wellhead'. In 1853, four people in the town died from cholera. Despite this water closets were still being emptied into the millstream. In 1894, a clean up was ordered, the water closets cut off and a sewage works built in 1900. The Witchell stretched from the stream to South Street, behind the gardens of the inns and houses of the High Street. It was used for grazing cattle and there was a small flint built stable for them to shelter in.

Around the crossroads the residents of Wendover continued their hardworking lives. Along Aylesbury Street, between numbers 7 and 9 the new fire station was built in 1877. Most buildings in the parish were vulnerable to fire being timber-framed with open fires and the voluntary firemen were kept busy. There were at least five fires on farms and at Wendover House, all the farm buildings were burned when a steam engine, used to thrash corn, caught fire. At Mr. Rose's barn north of the town though they saved a number of buildings from catching fire. It often took a long time to round up the horses to pull the engine, so they often grabbed the nearest horses available, even delaying stage coaches on occasions. In 1894, a new fire engine was bought by public subscription, but it was still horse-drawn.

The area now covered by Manor Road, Manor Crescent, Icknield Close and the school campus was Manor Farm. The Old Manor Farmhouse with its farmyard next door, where St. Anne's Close was built, was updated. To the west of the Aylesbury Road stood fields belonging to Vinetrees Farm, on the corner of which stood the windmill, built between 1796 and 1804 by John Phillips. He died in 1843, leaving it to his son Zachariah, who ran it until 1875, during which time it was powered solely by wind. Landowners from a wide area brought their wheat, oats, maize, peas and beans to be milled and it became a successful business. In 1875, Zachariah Phillips sold the mill for £1,000 to William Purssell, who farmed at Weston Turville. To augment the erratic source of natural power a steam engine was installed. A new engine house with a tall chimney was built and coal was brought by canal on barges owned by local coal merchant, Alfred Payne.

The canal, built in the 1790's was still an important means of transporting goods. Coal was needed by the cottagers to heat their homes and cook their food and by industries in the town. It arrived by barge and was off-loaded onto carts at the wharf from where they were pulled by horses along Wharf Road to the town. In 1868, a new gas works was built on the west side of the canal and the Wendover Gas Light and Coke Company was set up by the Vicar and Philip Smith, initially to light the church. Blacksmiths had always been an important part of the farming community. At the end of the 19th century, to meet

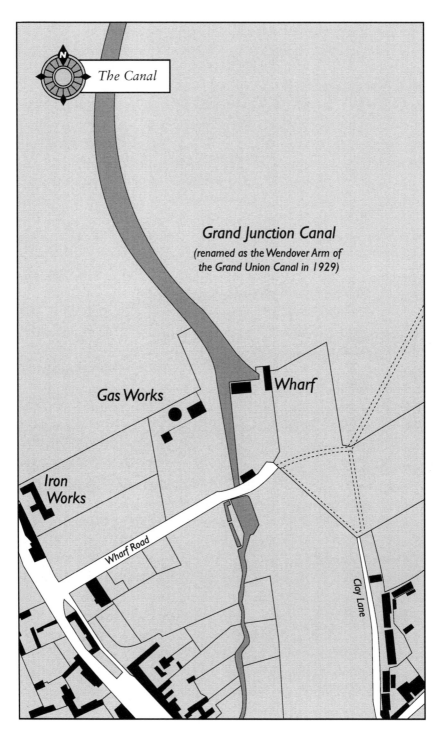

The Canal

Grand Junction Canal
*(renamed as the Wendover Arm of
the Grand Union Canal in 1929)*

Gas Works

Wharf

Iron
Works

Wharf Road

Clay Lane

even greater demands for metal products, the Chiltern Iron Works, run by Edwin Caudery, was built on the Aylesbury road where our health centre now stands. Further along were four cottages known as How's Housen but when they were acquired by the Rothschild family they were demolished and new cottages for their estate workers were built at Ashbrook.

Along the east side of Aylesbury Street were now a row of grand houses, home to the well-to-do residents of Wendover. Chiltern House had become the Chiltern House Academy, 'an academy for young gentlemen', run by Mr. Fuller. His successor was Mr. George Bushell, who was later appointed as head of the National School. Sturrick House, built originally as an open hall, was refurbished in 1820, becoming 'The New Inn' and in 1880 until the 1940's was run as 'The Temperance Hotel'. The Red House, which gained a new wing at this time, was used for many years as a doctor's surgery. In 1851 it was occupied by Doctor Joseph Savory, a GP, his wife, their seven children and three servants. Dr. Savory died in 1867 after more than forty years practice in Wendover. Number 20, known as Modbury, now Barclays Bank, was new and 'The George' had new bay windows installed and a new wrought iron sign. On the corner there was a baker's shop.

Next to the tannery in Tring Road was Holly House, owned by Mrs. Frances Anne Smith, widow of Abel Smith. The tanning industry ceased when Holly House became an infant school in 1828 until 1879, after which it was occupied by Alfred Payne, the coal and corn merchant. Schooling was neither compulsory nor free but there was a demand for infant education and the infant school had more pupils than the National School at one time. This was to be expected since fees were lower for infants and the older children could begin to earn wages from the age of ten. With their children at school, mothers could assist their husbands on the land or engage in lace making or the growing cottage industry of straw plaiting. As well as working hard on the farms and in the home, many people were engaged in cottage industries to supplement their incomes. Lace making had been introduced by Flemish and Huguenot refugees and lace dealers including a Mr. Atkins and a Mr. Dixon took the lace, a fashionable commodity, to London. Everybody wore hats in those days, plain ones to keep off the sun while working in the fields, better ones for church on Sundays. Most of the cottagers plaited straw for the Luton hat industry. Straw was collected after the harvest, flattened and plaited into very long strips, which were sold and taken to Luton to be made into hats, baskets and mats. On market day they carried the plait looped over their arms in lengths of twenty yards, known as a 'score'. A plaiter's income varied both seasonally and throughout the century but when the trade was at its peak, she could earn as much or more then a farm worker. Strawplaiting reached its peak in the nineteenth century as lacemaking declined. There were also some hat makers in Wendover.

As well as the cottages of Coldharbour and Casualty Row (York Buildings) and some newly built brick houses, there were now about thirty families living in Clay Lane. When 56 Clay Lane was built a straw plaiting school was held there. Children from the age of four were sent to learn to plait straw. The attendance at school of the older girls was affected by the market in straw plait. As late as 1868, the school records say 'the price of straw plait being raised the children are kept at home to plait'. Even when school attendance became compulsory in 1880, some children were sent to plait school in the evenings. At each end of Coldharbour there were two inns. 'The Nag's Head' stood at the lower end and 'The Packhorse' on the corner of Clay Lane. Joseph Fantham was a bargee who settled at 'The Packhorse', which was frequented by barge dwellers when the canal was in its heyday.

The first Congregational church had been built in 1811, just beyond Clay Lane, for thirty four members. By 1856, the membership had increased to 111 and a new church and school room were erected during the 1890's. In 1850, a new inn was built, known as 'The Four Seasons', which had rendered panels depicting Spring, Summer, Autumn and Winter. It later became known as 'The Rising Sun' and is now a restaurant. The tiny cottages called York Buildings housed large families in one up, one down accommodation, as the men who lived there were mostly farm labourers. Beyond York Buildings the road became a lane across fields to the right, where two more short terraces of cottages stood and in 1865 another inn 'The Rose and Crown' was built.

Common grazing lands occupied the south side of Tring Road. Boddington Hill was enclosed in November 1857 and ten acres were transferred to Halton Parish. Twenty allotments were awarded to various persons and four acres awarded to the Churchwardens and Overseers of the Poor of the Parish as a recreational ground. Being on a slope at the top of the hill, the Parish did not consider them as suitable for a recreation ground and they were exchanged for four acres on the Aylesbury road, owned by Mr. Lionel de Rothschild, which have become Ashbrook or Castle Park.

The road was still narrow but there were a number of cottages on the south side plus Bank Farm and Brook House, which in 1881 was the home of Doctor Edward Odling GP, and his family. There was still a working watermill, the Nether Mill, on the original millstream worked by the ladies of the Hoare family, Isabella, Elizabeth and Anne, for many years. They lived at Paradise House where, from 1850 – 1870, they ran a boarding school for young ladies in buildings adapted from what remained of a convent on the site. The mill was later acquired by Mr. Joseph Senior Holland who was also proprietor of 'The Red Lion Commercial and Family Hotel', and of the Wendover Brewery and Malt House, as well as a builder and contractor. Where Heronpath House now stands was Bucksbridge Farmhouse and its fields beyond. The Saunders family, who farmed there for many generations, supplied the horses for the horse-drawn fire engine. They preferred to live at Sluice Cottage, which still had a millpond beside it, but this has since dried up. By Sluice Cottage, there used to be a stile and a public footpath, now closed. The Wellhead Spring was still visible above the ground in the 1850's and in winter it flooded the road. The Canal Company culverted it along the edge of Manor House Park, past Sluice Cottage, along Witchell and under the school playground, eventually emerging at the wharf. The Hampden Pond had been created by the Canal Company in the 1790's and became popular for ice skating when it froze over in the winter. Sadly, in 1868, it was the scene of a tragic accident. A number of boys from the National School, taking advantage of a half-holiday in January, went to play on the frozen pond, the ice broke and five of the schoolboys were drowned despite brave attempts to rescue them.

The incline in the London Road, just past Wellhead Lane, has been known as Church Hill, Workhouse Hill and Gravel Pit Hill. There is said to have been a workhouse or union house near the top of this hill on the east side of the road. There was a row of cottages called the Ten Housen beyond Road Barn, to house the poor but from about 1840 onwards, the poor were sent to the workhouse at Bledlow. At the junction of Wellhead Lane and London Road there was a tollgate until 1876.

As well as working hard, the closeknit community of Wendover has always known how to enjoy itself, satisfied with simple pleasures. The fairs in May and October were great social occasions and cricket matches were regarded as important events with much excitement and refreshments served. There were May Day dances and school treats, often accompanied by the local brass band. There was also a good drum and fife band. For many years there was a show and ploughing match held annually in the fields behind 'The Red Lion' by the Chiltern Hills Agricultural Association. Farmers from all over the district attended the show followed by a sumptuous dinner and music in the evening. There were Harvest Home suppers to celebrate the end of the farming year.

National and royal events have always been celebrated. For Queen Victoria's Jubilee in 1887, there was a procession to St. Mary's Church for a special service, a dinner for all adult cottagers, a tea for all children under twelve and a bonfire on Bacombe Hill. Nine hundred people dined together in the meadow at the back of 'The Red Lion'. Due to a shortage of tents, a 'marquee' was constructed using scaffold poles, rick cloths and ropes lent by local builders and farmers. Great joints of meat were roasted or boiled the day before and served cold, with hot potatoes cooked in big boilers, followed by hot plum puddings, which had been boiled in a very large copper. The day finished with games, dancing and fireworks.

9

Sundays

1837 – 1901 AD

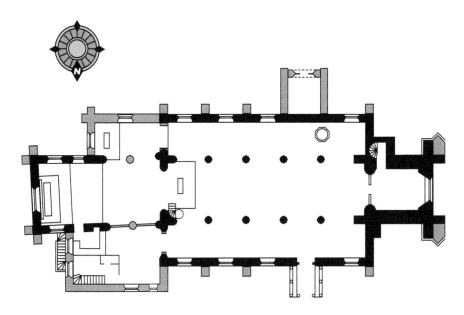

St Mary's Church

A fter a week of working hard on the farms and in the town, most
people walked to church on Sundays, along the Heron Path.
St. Mary's Church has stood in its perfect setting since Norman
times. The changes in its layout have happened gradually, due to the
transition from Catholic to Protestant worship. After a period of
neglect, the new vicar in 1837, the Reverend Spencer Thornton, found
St. Mary's in serious need of refurbishment. His uncle, Abel Smith,
the Lord of the Manor, and other parishioners agreed to finance the
work inside and outside and to provide additional seating and an
organ. The church was closed from August until November in 1839
to enable this to be carried out. The well known London architect,
Edward Buckton Lamb, designed a new octagonal font with a carved
oak cover. The elaborate rood screen, which separated the chancel
from the nave, survived until 1842, being of historical interest.

The Reverend Albert Smith, son of Abel Smith and brother of
Philip Smith, became vicar in 1867. Like Thornton, he was young
and energetic and, having just graduated from Oxford, was eager
to update St. Mary's in line with the revived forms of liturgy of the
Church of England that stemmed from the Oxford Movement. This
time the Diocesan Architect George Edmund Street was chosen for the
task. In 1868 he would have found St. Mary's looking very different
from its appearance today. All the walls were covered with plaster
between brick buttresses, the shallow nave roof was almost invisible
from the ground and there were sash windows in the clerestory. The
main entrance was by the south door through a timber porch. A
coach drive lined with trees ran through the churchyard, leading to
the vicarage, which stood between the church and the Manor House.
Internally, the church had plaster ceilings painted to represent oak.
There were galleries for the gentry and their servants on the north and
south sides of the nave, with private staircases to each, the servants
sitting at the back and the gentry in front. There were pegs on which

to hang the gentlemen's top hats. The rest of the congregation sat in high-backed seats down the middle. There was also a gallery at the west end, erected as a place for the choir and band of instrumentalists and later used for the organ. Under this stood the font. In the centre of the nave, just below the chancel arch stood a double-decker pulpit. The preacher stood above while the clerk kept a watchful eye on the congregation from the seat below him.

The church closed in May 1868 and services were held in Thomas Croxford's barn, part of the Manor Farm in Aylesbury Street, alongside the path to Vinetrees. Meanwhile, the church was transformed. All the exterior walls were refaced in flint with Bath stone dressings and the buttresses rebuilt. The whole of the upper part of the nave was rebuilt with square windows in the clerestory and new high-pitched roofs built over the nave and chancel. Practically all the window tracery was replaced or recarved. On the tower, new battlements and a lead-covered spirelet were added. The old porches were removed and new ones built and the main entrance changed from the south to the north side. The church was the first building in the town to use gas.

The galleries, staircases and high-backed pews were all swept away to make room for new oak seating for 396 adults plus 130 children, who had smaller spaces under the tower and the new south chancel aisle. The 17th Century memorial slabs in the chancel floor were resited under the tower and the chancel floor, then paved with decorative tiles while plainer tiles were used throughout the rest of the church. A new organ was installed in a newly created organ chamber north of the chancel and the choir took their places in the chancel. Lamb's font is now outside in the churchyard having been replaced by one designed by Street and carved in stone from Caen in Normandy.

The vicar Albert Smith and his brother Philip were the main contributors to the expense of the work. After the great opening ceremony on the 1st June 1869, they continued to beautify the church. In 1871, Philip gave the attractive oak lychgate and in 1874, Philip and Albert gave a new reredos. In 1875 a new pulpit dedicated to the memory of the Reverend Charles Champneys, Albert's predecessor as vicar, was provided.

The Smith family also donated several stained glass windows. Robert, an older brother, gave the large east window with Philip donating the windows on the north and south walls of the chancel. In 1886, Albert gave the oak screen in the tower arch as a memorial to his mother, Frances Anne Smith, and the area below the tower became a vestry. From 1886 to 1895, further windows were installed by members of the Smith family. Between 1896 and 1899, the series of windows depicting angels were added by other residents of Wendover.

The oak lychgate

10

The Manor House

1837 – 1901 AD

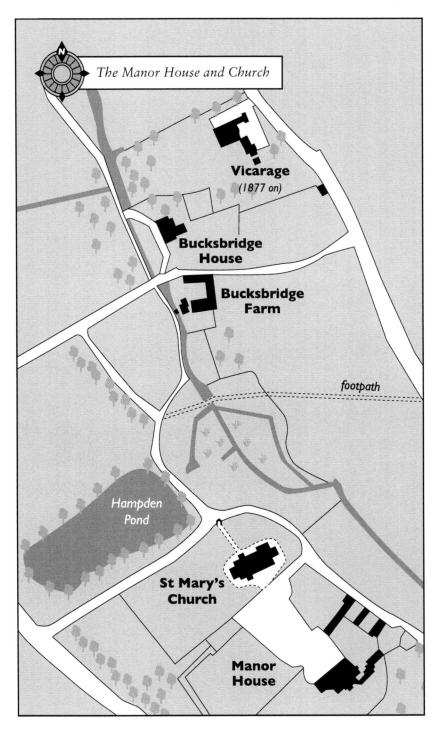

The Manor House and Church

Vicarage
(1877 on)

Bucksbridge
House

Bucksbridge
Farm

footpath

Hampden
Pond

St Mary's
Church

Manor
House

Back in the twelfth century, rectorial rights to the church in Wendover were granted to the Priory of St. Mary Overy in Southwark, in London. To the south of the church there was a parsonage for the use of the representative of the Priory, and a vicarage for the local priest, but by Victorian times the parsonage was redundant.

The Manor House, Wendover House, was built on the site of the former parsonage in the 1850's. The 1851 census shows us that it was occupied by Lt. General James Watson, aged 70, his wife and son, and their servants. The vicarage was occupied by the Reverend Charles Champneys, aged 37, and his wife. Between 1871 and 1873, the Manor House was almost entirely rebuilt for Philip Smith, the Lord of the Manor, in modest Elizabethan style, with a service wing in old brick to match the 18th century stable block. Philip was a captain in the Grenadier Guards and, therefore, did not spend a great deal of time in Wendover, but his brother Albert became the vicar in 1867 and spent the rest of his life here. He was the last vicar to live in the old vicarage, which was approached by a narrow road from London Road. After the rebuilding of the Manor House, Albert and his family took up residence there and the old vicarage was demolished.

A new vicarage was built on part of Bucksbridge Farm in 1877 and named Winterton House. It was designed by Dewey in the Elizabethan style. In the 1881 census, eight members of Albert's family, plus seven servants, are listed as residents of the Manor House, but soon after they moved to the new vicarage and the Manor House was let to a family called Godwin.

Philip had an active and distinguished military career, serving in Canada, Gibraltar and Egypt. On his return from Egypt in November 1882, he was given a hero's welcome by the people of Wendover.

The town had been profusely decorated with evergreens, flags and bunting. He was met at Aylesbury by his brother Albert and their carriage was accompanied by three Wendover boys, George Jeffray, Tom Beeson and George Dell, who were drummers in his regiment. A procession of local dignitaries, musical bands, local tradesmen, tenants and friends assembled. As they reached the Clock Tower, they were met by the National School children and the church choir, singing 'Home Sweet Home'. They joined the procession and marched along the High Street and London Road to the Manor House where the Colonel lived.

Philip went on to become a Lieutenant General at the age of 55, but he died two years later. His duties as Lord of the Manor are obvious from the many legacies he left behind. At that time, landowners spent vast sums of money on their estates. Philip Smith used his inherited wealth to beautify Wendover. Firstly, he had the Literary Institute built as a memorial to his father, a valuable asset to the town for many years. In 1869 he gave the land on which to build a new school, which served the children and adults of Wendover until 1974. At the same time, he and his brother Albert contributed generously to the extensive restoration of St. Mary's Church. In 1870, Philip was instrumental in the extension of the market hall into the imposing Clock Tower we have today. This well-liked Lord of the Manor died on 1st November 1894. At the funeral at St. Mary's, his coffin was borne by eight guardsmen in their scarlet tunics and bearskins. He was succeeded as Lord of the Manor by his brother Albert.

11

The End of an Era

1837 – 1901 AD

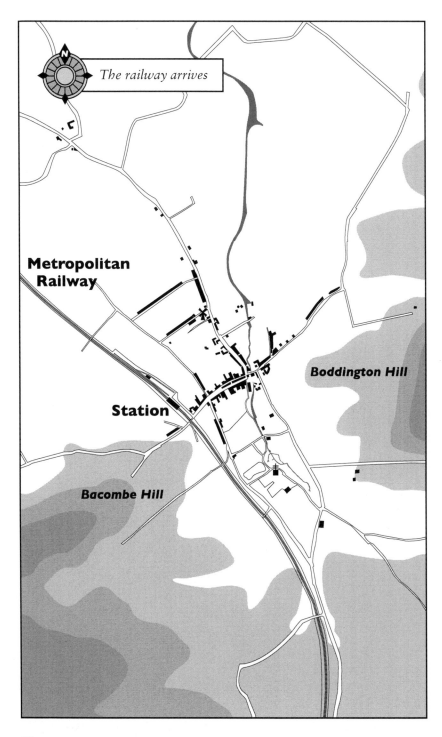

The railway arrives

Metropolitan
Railway

Station

Boddington Hill

Bacombe Hill

Until 1892, most residents of Wendover hardly ever left Wendover. Up to that time, the mode of travel to London by train was from Tring or Princes Risborough, which could only be reached by coach or on foot. But life was about to change, brought about by the building of the Metropolitan Railway from London to Aylesbury.

At a special ceremony on 21st March 1890, the Lord of the Manor, Colonel Philip Smith, cut the first turf out of Long Piece using a brand new spade, which is still kept at the Clock Tower. Excavators called steam navvies were used to dig a deep cutting on the London side of the top of Pound Street. The railway station was built to a standard design by Charles Liddell for the Metropolitan Railway. The railway opened officially on 1st September 1892, a day of outstanding importance to the people of Wendover. There was a procession led by a band from the school to Marshallsays Meadow, part of Lime Tree Farm, and now the area occupied by Forest Close and Coombe Avenue. There was a big public tea and sports to mark the occasion, followed by a celebration dinner at 'The Red Lion'.

The building of the railway made it much easier for Wendover people to travel to other places and also made it easy for people from elsewhere to visit Wendover. This led to the development of commuter traffic and an increased demand for new houses. From that time onwards the town spread beyond the Borough with many houses being built, initially along the Aylesbury Road, Chiltern Road, Perry Street and Dobbins Lane. Mr. Alfred de Rothschild lived at his mansion, Halton House. When the railway opened a constant stream of celebrities arrived at Wendover Station, where they were met with magnificent carriages in dark blue and yellow livery. Estate servants were stationed at every corner and after dark each held a lantern to light the way. The guests' personal servants stayed at 'The Shoulder of Mutton' inn, which was renamed 'The Railway Hotel'.

Up to this time, goods of all kinds were carried to and from Wendover either by great road wagons or by barges on the Grand Junction Canal. The railway altered all this and Mr. Alfred Payne, coal and corn merchant of Holly House, Tring Road, transferred his business to the railway goods yard, becoming the official agent for delivery of goods brought by rail.

A popular event was the annual Flower Show held in the grounds of the Manor House. Besides the show of flowers, fruit and vegetables, there was a cricket match and other sports as well as outdoor concerts and competitions. Wendover and Chiltern Hills Agricultural Show, held in the meadow next to Witchell, was later moved to Halton as part of Alfred Rothschild's hospitality. His generosity affected many lives. At his expense a soup kitchen was set up in a small brick building behind the Congregational Church in Tring Road, with bread supplied by local bakers. Twice a year, at Christmas and his birthday in July, he sent gifts of money to every child and member of staff at Wendover School.

Charitable acts have long been a feature of Wendover life. In Thomas Hill's will of 1723, two greatcoats were donated every winter until 1916, and in 1844 Robert Fox gave 60 jackets for the poor. The Provident and Dorcas Society supplied blankets and bedding. In the very severe winter of 1895, grocery tickets were distributed to those in need.

As the nineteenth century closed this country was at war with South Africa. In March 1900, the 'Relief of Ladysmith' being an important victory in the war, all the children were given an orange to celebrate, an orange being a special treat in 1900. Wendover was still largely a farming community but the arrival of the railway was already changing the nature of the town. The place was expanding as more people wanted to live here. Local shops and businesses were thriving. There were butchers, bakers, grocers, drapers, tailors, builders, carters, coal dealers, blacksmiths and saddlers and even a watchmaker and jeweller and tea-rooms. Public affairs were governed by the Wendover Parish Council, whose first meeting took place in 1894, under the leadership of its chairman, the Reverend Albert Smith. The Victorian era ended on 22nd January 1901, with the death of Queen Victoria. She was 82 years old and had reigned for 64 years.

Many images of Wendover at the end of the Victorian period and early years of the 20th century are in 'Wendover in Old Picture Postcards' by Colin J. Seabright.

In the 1960's a number of elderly residents were interviewed and their memories of the final years of the 19th Century recorded. Although unfortunately these reminiscences are not credited, they provide a fascinating first-hand account of what life was like in Wendover at the time:

"Round about 1885 Wendover was still a small village, standing on Boddington Hill. In summer one could see very few buildings. The valley was predominately cornfields. In the evening the hillside would be alive with glow worms. In the village the cottagers would put up their wooden shutters. The cottages were lit with paraffin lamps and candles. Mr. Blow and Mr. Billy Meade would put out the street lamps at 10 p.m. Before them other people did it. A lamp was put on a bracket of a cottage in Clay Lane.

There were cottages along Tring Road on either side of the 'Rose and Crown Inn'. The Café was in those days a saw mill owned by Mr. Gamble. Mr. Simmonds and one son worked there. Mr. Simmonds' wife kept the 'Rose and Crown', and moved into one of the Roseneath Cottages later. Their daughter, Mrs. Eggleton, lived in another of these cottages with her husband and four daughters. The cottages are small, each comprising a small living room opening onto the road, with a door leading into a tiny back kitchen. From here are stairs up to the two small bedrooms and a door out to the yard (with outside toilet), and garden.

The cooking was done on the fire. A big pot would be hung above the fire and the vegetables, each sort in a 'potato sock' would be cooked together. The potato socks were made of string mesh. Some women would make their own using a wooden peg held between the toes and a ball of string, the bag being woven on the foot. In Wendover a woman came round selling the socks and many bought from her.

In the living room of her cottage old Mrs. Simmonds held a plaiting school for about eight children. The straw was brought in bundles and the plaits would be collected weekly by Mrs. Goodson of Aston Clinton. The plaits went to Luton for the hat factories. Men came door to door selling hats.

A mill for pressing and splitting the straws was fastened to the wall. The straw was made into complicated patterns, rapidly woven. Mrs. Eggleton had a hook on her wall to which the end of the plait would be fastened to stretch it. Plaiting was a popular occupation and children found it a pleasant pastime. In 1850 there was a plaiting school at the bottom of Clay Lane run by Mrs. Dancer.

In one of the cottages on the other side of the Inn lived Mrs. Radcliffe. In her front room beneath the window stood a table. Here would be laid home-made sweets and the children would run in on their way to school. Favourite sweet of all was 'Hanky Panky', similar to chewing gum and costing one farthing for a strip about three inches long. Mrs. Radcliffe spent most of her time at her lace pillow, just leaving off to attend to customers. Some cottagers would sell Treacle Dabs the size of a crown, one farthing each.

The children went to school for the whole day, paying one or two pence per week depending on their fathers' occupation. The tiny boys in the Infants from two years old, wore petticoats, not trousers. The girls always wore white goffered aprons. Slates and pencils were used. A boy used to ring the first bell at 8.45am. When the 9am bell rang the children had to line up – girls together and boys together. They sung as they marched into school. 'Order, Order, Cherish Order, Saves Both Time and Toil'.

The Headmaster, Mr. Bushell, was liked and respected. He was a big man and used snuff frequently. He was a good disciplinarian but seldom needed to use his stick. When Mr. Bushell punished one boy the others kept out of his way! He had several daughters and one son, Jack, who all enjoyed singing and there were great concerts. His youngest daughter is said to have died from fever after being scratched by her pet cat.

When the Vicar came to school the girls had to stand and curtsey. The boys had to stand.

In winter skating was a happy pastime. Some children would skate on Hampden Pond during their dinner hour. An uncle would bring the Eggleton's children dinner to school to save them from going home. When Halton Reservoir froze (not very often), the band would be there. Unemployed men from Aylesbury would be there with chairs and the ladies and girls would pay the men to put on and fasten their skating boots.

After school and during the holidays there were always plenty of things to do. Of course each child would be expected to help at home, cleaning the boots, cleaning knives and forks etc. There was time to play too. They played 'Doddies' with marbles, whips and tops, dabbers, bowled iron hoops for boys, wooden hoops for girls. Nip, catch and conjure (a bit like cricket) and ran races.

Boddington Hill was then a grassy slope, cropped by sheep. The girls would climb up there gathering grasses with red berries, called Jingle Bells, and orchids, wild berries, strawberries or blackberries in season. Elder bloom and red poppy leaves and poppy heads could be sold to Mrs. Eames who lived in Clay Lane, for three farthings per pound. Poppy heads were sometimes boiled with camomile flowers and pulped, and this was then applied as a soporific fomentation for neuralgia or toothache.

Peacocks Farm on the top of Boddington Hill was a fine sight. The peacocks could be heard in the village. The farm belonged to the Rothschilds of Aston Clinton. Mr. Benning remembers when a fire broke out there about 50 years ago. Wendover Fire Brigade set out with horse and cart. They were unable to get up Boddington Hill and had to approach via The Hale. When they finally arrived more than four hours later the fire was out! After that a pump was put in at the Wharf (off Wharf Road) with the intention of pumping up sufficient water to the farm but it was unsatisfactory. Finally, water was piped from Aston Clinton. The farm was demolished about 50 years ago.

A Mr. Holland had 'The Red Lion' at that time. His coachman, a Mr. Radcliffe, who lived where the Spinning Wheel Café is now, could be hired out with the barouche to take people out to entertainments, weddings, etc. It was considered to be a rare treat to ride in the barouche behind Mr. Radcliffe with his top hat!

Even in the poor families there was sufficient to eat and clothes were kept clean. Of course the girls were taught to sew and crochet at an early age, as there were insufficient vacancies for those who would have liked to be apprenticed to the village dressmaker.

The children would glean round the cornfields after the harvest. The ears of corn thus garnered would be taken to be thrashed by flail in Geofrey's Yard (where Brax is now) then to the Mill House (by the village school), and this would provide flour for the families' bread. The topping from the corn would be fed to the family pig. Most families had at least one pig. Two sisters remember two pet pigs, from a big litter who were reared on the bottle. These piglets would trot around after the girls, lying on the hearth rug or going for walks, and would race after the girls if called. When one had to go to the butchers it refused to go until Mrs. Eggleton took it, the pig trotting after her down the road! A sad day!

There were lots of treats too. Lady Battersy of Aston Clinton was very keen on Temperance Work and on Temperance Day there would be a treat in her garden. The young people belonging to the Band of Hope in Wendover once travelled there in a decorated barge, from the Wharf. The School Drum and Fife Band were in the horse-drawn barge and off they went singing lustily. Often it would be 'We're out on the Ocean Sailing'! The girls, of course, would wear their long gloves, hats with veils, and carry beautiful parasols. One memorable day a certain Fred Bedford who had been unable to get on at the Wharf, hurried along to the bridge, and as the barge sailed underneath, leapt amongst them. Needless to say they made room for him then.

There were treats with the Congregational Sunday School. Sometimes these would be to Ashridge Monument. A gaily decorated wagon drawn by two horses would take them. Besides donkeys there were also stags by the monument. Sometimes they went to West Wycombe. Frequently the treat would be at the Castle House, along Aylesbury Road. Mr. Yorke, the Congregational Minister lived there. The procession would be led by the Wendover Brass Band and three donkeys. Swings would be hung on the walnut trees in the garden, and there would be races and donkey rides and, of course, tea. Each child took their own mug. At the end every child would be given an orange and a bag of sweets.

Sometimes the children would go to the Vicarage for the Day School treat, near Winterton House, at the invitation of the Vicar, the Reverend Smith. First they had a service, and after at the vicarage there would be the similar treats, but would also include dancing on the lawns. The band was paid £2 between them.

Colonel Godwin lived at the Manor House, and was much respected. There was a passage from the Manor House into the church.

The young ladies hats in those days were usually magnificent. They could be made of chiffon with veiling, feathers and broaches. They wore fishus round their necks, and very full dresses with big petticoats. The dress would be held up a little at each side as the lady walked and often the hems of the lovely top petticoat would show. Shoes were sometimes worn of an evening but buttoned boots were more usually worn, or boots with elastic sides. In hot weather parasols were always carried.

Most of the oldest Wendover people now living here attended the Congregational Church. A typical Sunday for Mr. and Mrs. Eggleton's family would be like this:

Sunday School from 9am until 10.30am. Then the children would go into the church gallery for morning service.

At mid-day they would walk home to dinner.

In the afternoon there would be Sunday School at 2pm.

Then a walk with Father to visit Granny Eggleton at Addington Cottages and home to tea.

Church again from 6pm to 7pm with Mother, and then home to a sing-song around the piano (to which friends usually came).

At the time of Queen Victoria's Diamond Jubilee the school had a treat at Wytchell and Holland's Meadow. There was tea, races and games and Mr. Bushell presented each child with a commemorative mug.

Mr. Rothschild tried to close Boddington Hill but people pulled fences down and he had to give it up.

The Attorney General of the Liberal Government Lawson Warton tried to close part of Bacombe but was stopped the same way.

Sturrick House used to be the New Inn, then became a Temperance Hotel.

The Canal used to bring coal to Wendover and hay and straw went back to Paddington. Coal was distributed as far as Amersham.

The windmill was used for grinding corn, but there was plenty of work too for the water mill.

The gas works, by the gasometer, used to supply enough for Wendover. Now of course it is piped from Aylesbury, to our gasometer.

The Oddfellows club feast used to be at Hampden Meadows. A greasy pole would be put up and a leg of mutton placed on the end. The one who could get it kept it! A greasy pig would be released in the crowds, and whoever caught it, kept it!"

12

Turbulent Times

1901 to the Present Day

Turbulent Times

In Kelly's Directory for 1903 Wendover was described as a town and parish set in the Chiltern Hills with a railway station on the Metropolitan extension railway with the great Central Railway running through. The town was still supplied with water from natural springs. The Wendover Arm of the Grand Junction Canal was no longer in use but the gas works by the canal established in 1868 still supplied gas and the streets were lit with gas lamps. The roads were still made from flints, not metalled and were sandy and dusty. There was a police station run by Sergeant William White and a fire station with a volunteer fire brigade of twelve men led by Alfred William Dancer.

The population of the town was now over two thousand plus another eighteen hundred in the ecclesiastical parish. The parish was part of the rural deanery of Wendover, the archdeaconry of Buckingham and the diocese of Oxford. The living was in the gift of the Lord Chancellor. There was also a Congregational Chapel, a Baptist Chapel, a Primitive Methodist Chapel and a Mission Hall. There was a school for four hundred pupils with strong links with St. Mary's Church and a school for thirty children at Scrubs Wood. The local GP Dr. Edwin Goodburn Woollerton was appointed Medical Officer for the district in 1907. Nursing care was provided by the Nursing Association, the nurse visiting her patients by bicycle.

The building of the railway in 1892 had changed the way of life in Wendover but an even greater change was still to come. At the beginning of the twentieth century, the grounds of the Manor House were the location of the annual Wendover Flower Show, always held on the first Tuesday in August. In 1914, torrential rain came and the show was all but abandoned. That night, at eleven o'clock, war was declared and the calm, rural life of Wendover would never be the same again. In 1913 soldiers had marched through the town and aeroplanes began to pass overhead but now this rural retreat became a great military centre with guns and equipment being transported through the streets. The training camp under canvas built on the hillside at Halton for Kitcheners Army overshadowed the community and made the town extremely vulnerable to attack.

The streets of Wendover were full of soldiers from the camp and on Sundays there was an influx of their visitors arriving by train. The hotels were full, many houses were rented out and the shops increased their trade. New industries such as laundries started to serve the camp. So, as well as changing the atmosphere of Wendover, the war brought prosperity to the town. Until then Wendover was always referred to as a town but it became known as "the village" by the soldiers from Halton and the practice has continued.

The vicar in 1914 was the Reverend J. Holding. He created a new Parish Magazine at this time, a non-sectarian paper designed for everyone to read. There were open air services on Witchell Meadow for soldiers and their families. In the school playground a YMCA hut was erected for use by the soldiers. There was a bar, gramophone records, concerts and entertainments. Princess Victoria officially opened it in June 1915. A billiards table, which had been installed upstairs in the Literary Institute in 1911, was put to good use by the soldiers.

A recruitment drive in the school playground resulted in many local young men joining up in a mood of patriotic fervour. Those left behind were involved in the War Effort. The Recruiting and General Purposes Sub-Committee organised parcels for men at the front. The Red Cross Working Party produced warm underwear, socks and other comforts to fill the parcels. Copies of the new parish magazine were sent and enjoyed by the local recruits. Gifts of fruit and vegetables were taken to the Manor House from where Mr. Routh distributed them to the navy. New laid eggs were collected by the school children to be sent to the wounded. They also harvested belladonna and foxgloves to be sold to make drugs for the wounded and make money for the Prisoners' War Fund. In the autumn of 1917 they collected blackberries to make jam for the navy and conkers to make explosives. In November there were two tons of conkers stored at the windmill.

With their men gone to war, the women of Wendover took on the farming work and at home life was difficult. A complete blackout at night, enforced by special constables, was introduced. The gas street lights were not lit during the war and the town clock did not strike. On 1st October 1916 two zeppelins lit up the sky above Boddington Hill and the report in the parish magazine read "beautiful and awe-inspiring. All the colours of the rainbow, with a preponderance of rosy pink were reflected in the mackerel sky". Wendover's beautiful woods were felled to provide props for the trenches on the battlefields, a light railway being built to transport the logs to Wendover station.

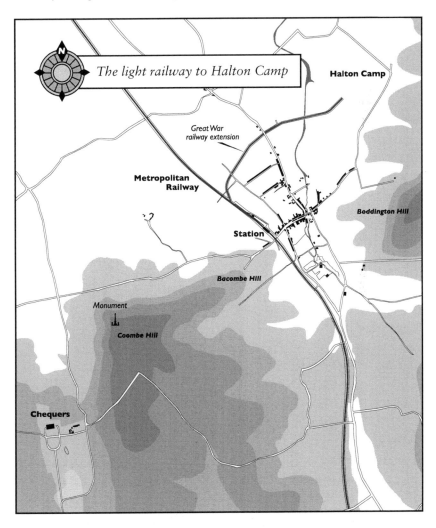

The light railway to Halton Camp

No bombs fell on Wendover during the Great War but the town was scarred by those four awful years. Over fifty local men perished, their loss keenly felt by all in such a small community, not least at the school where many had been pupils. On 11th November 1918, the shops were closed and the children off school. At eleven o'clock the hooters at the iron works and the sawmill sounded followed by two minutes silent. The war was over.

Between the two world wars came the Depression when the farming industry declined. There were once nine farmhouses in the town itself but these have all disappeared now except one, Bank Farm in Tring Road. There are still other farms in the Forrens. In 1944 the Chiltern Hills Agricultural Society was still going strong with an annual ploughing match and competitions for rick building, thatching, hedging and ditching and for the best growing crops and roots. The big agricultural hiring fairs became pleasure fairs full of roundabouts, traction engines and Romany caravans.

However the railway had made Wendover into a popular tourist attraction bringing prosperity to many tradespeople. The 1920s and 1930s saw great development especially along the railway. In 1923 we still had a lamplighter but by 1927 electric street lamps had been installed supplied by the power station in Aylesbury. The Red Rose Garage in Aylesbury Road started operating local bus services in the early twenties and by 1930 ran several buses a day to Aylesbury, Chesham, High Wycombe, Oxford and London. There were sixteen public houses plus a British Legion Club serving a population of five thousand plus visitors to the town.

Just as life was improving after the Depression the country was plunged into the Second World War. With RAF Halton so close on one side and Chequers, the country retreat of the Prime Minister, on the other, Wendover again felt vulnerable. RAF Halton was now well hidden amongst woodland but searchlight and anti aircraft detachments were established in the surrounding hills. The Monument on top of Coombe Hill was camouflaged to prevent it from becoming a useful landmark for the enemy, so close to Chequers, and it survived the war undamaged. Road signs were removed or turned round to confuse possible invaders. A complete blackout from half an hour before sunset operated, policed by ARP Wardens. There were air raid shelters in the school playground and a few in private gardens but most people sheltered in cellars or under the kitchen table. The air raid warning was a siren followed by the all clear. Gas masks had to be worn and were distributed from the British Legion Hall in Chiltern Road. Enemy bombers could be seen and heard flying over from France to the industrial Midlands but the only bomb dropped here was near St. Mary's Church and thought to be an accidental drop.

Wendover's agricultural background was invaluable in the war effort. In a place where there had always been plenty of food there was food rationing. Meat was rationed so families kept chickens at home and looked for extra food in the wild. Fruit and vegetables were only available in season such as potatoes, onions and leeks in winter. People went out into the countryside to collect wild raspberries, blackberries, nuts and mushrooms. The school garden was turned into a "Victory Plot" and the Wendover Horticultural and Produce Association set up "Dig for Victory" in the community.

Wendover became the temporary home of many evacuees from London and southeast England. Some were housed at the Manor House and others at the vicarage, Winterton House, but most were accommodated in ordinary family homes. The school took in over 130 children mainly from Ealing and their teachers. Their school dinners were cooked in the Baptist Chapel. Londoners travelled out to Wendover to catch a few hours undisturbed sleep in the countryside. Witchell Meadow within easy reach of the railway station was a popular choice. The evacuees almost all returned to their own homes as soon as it was felt that the main danger was over.

Twenty two men from Wendover sacrificed their lives during the Second World War. Their names are recorded on the War Memorial on the Manor Waste. The rest of Wendover was fortunate as it was not bombed or invaded as feared. When VE Day was announced in May 1945, there was great rejoicing, the school was closed for two days and street parties were organised to celebrate. Following the war everyday life returned to what it had been in 1939. No longer an active farming community, many of the fields became housing estates bringing many newcomers to the area especially from Middlesex as Metroland expanded. They found the peace they were seeking except on Sunday 21st May 1950, when a tornado hit the area. The tornado struck Wendover just before 5pm lifting the roof off a barn at Wendover Dean, damaging the roof of the Baptist Chapel and tearing up huge elms in Witchell Meadow. Roaring down the High Street it damaged the butcher's shop, 'The Red Lion', the newsagent's and the Literary Institute. A large tree in the school playground was ripped out and the top floor of 'The George' badly damaged. It demolished trees and outhouses in the gardens of Aylesbury Road before spiralling across to RAF Halton lifting aircraft off the airfield like kites.

A bypass for Wendover was first proposed in 1937 to connect Dobbins Lane with Aylesbury Road near Worlds End. Then the war came and plans for the road were shelved. However, with the further expansion of the village and the increased use of the motor car, the main route through the High Street was becoming a bottleneck. The problem was revisited in the 1960s but a bypass rejected mainly on the grounds of cost. There were plans to demolish Pound Street and the buildings at the bottom of the High Street including the Literary Institute but to leave the Clock Tower in the middle of a roundabout. These plans and others were halted by the intervention of the Wendover Society whose aim was and still is 'to preserve the existing beauties of the village and to do its best to see that any future developments would be good developments in keeping with the character of Wendover'. In 1985, after consultation by questionnaire between the County engineers and the public, a route was chosen which closely followed the railway line on land owned by British Rail or the County Council. At long last, due greatly to the efforts of Councillor Frank Goodson, the bypass was opened in 1997, relieving to an extent the pressure on the High Street. Once again the nature of Wendover has been shaped by the effects of a means of transport.

Wendover Station, built 1892

The Shoulder of Mutton, formerly The Railway Hotel

No.1, High Street

Edwardian shop front

13

Urban Village

1901 to the Present Day

Urban Village

By 1900 the High Street was established as a thriving commercial area supplying a wide variety of goods and services to the population of Wendover and its surroundings. The department store Freeman's continued trading well into the 20th century. In 1915, after the death of the postmaster Mr. Freeman senior, the Post Office was moved to South Street. The space left became the ladies' fashion department. The section on the left which had housed Mr. Freeman's trap was converted to a gentlemen's outfitters. They also sold agricultural clothing which they delivered to the outlying villages and their farmworkers. The chemist department was later run by Mr. Sargent and Mr. Cresswell. Mr. Sargent owned the house behind which had a large room with a grand piano used for piano examinations and a dancing school run by his daughters Yvette and Daphne.

In competition with Freemans was another department store on the opposite side of the High Street. The double-fronted shop was run by Mr. Edwin King and his daughters at the turn of the century. In the early 1900's it was a draper's shop called Nicholas Lee which did good business selling blinds and blackout curtains during the First World War. It also sold clothing, stationery, tobacco and cigarettes and became known as 'the blouse shop.' At one time it was called Tailors which sold all sorts of goods including boots and shoes. Between the wars it was run by Mr. and Mrs. Edwards. Over the shop there was a beautiful flat with a balcony at the front. Unfortunately the flat had very uneven floors so Mr. Edwards, who had been a ship's carpenter, made bespoke furniture to fit. Later it was run by Mr and Mrs Bell who sold clothing and haberdashery. Towards the latter part of the century it became 'Biddies', an expensive ladies' fashion shop and is now called 'Time' which sells gentlemen's clothes as well. Part of the premises is Ivan Cammack's the Opticians.

There have been several butcher's shops. The How family had run a butchery business linked with Wellwick Farm at 1 High Street since the Napoleonic Wars. It became famous for its sausages made to a secret recipe. Fred Caudery had a butcher's shop between 'The Red Lion' and Lloyd's Bank. Albert Goodson, who later had his own shop in Pound Street, was his assistant. This shop became W.Smith and Sons. By the 1970's it was a fruit shop and butcher's side by side called Sidney Stevens and Son. It is now a barber's shop and the @ St Mary's Church shop. When King's Head Parade was built in the 1960's there was a butcher's shop called Tilbury's on the end by the library entrance. In the early half of the century there was a wet fish shop called Spittles which also sold game including pheasants and hares. There was a Macfisheries at one time and then some of the butchers sold fresh fish but now fish can only be bought in Budgen's supermarket, except on Thursdays when there is a market stall.

Hogarth House was for many years a greengrocer's shop. Mr George Brackley grew many of the vegetables on the land at the back of the shop and the adjacent path leading to Witchell was known as Brackley's Path. In the 1930's the shop was run by the Misses Brackley. In the 1970's it was occupied by Brown and Merry before becoming a shop selling maps and prints and then Sally Turner's Antiques. King's Head Parade included a greengrocer's shop called Jerome's.

There was a choice of grocery shops. Pearce Brothers ran their grocery and hardware store for many years in the part of the premises which is now the Chinese Restaurant. The wet fish shop and a greengrocer's were next door. Pearce Brothers became Essex and Company and then the International Stores in the 1960's. At the beginning of the century a family called Blake owned several shops in the town. The shop on the corner of Dobbins Lane and Pound Street was Blake's becoming Seago's and Kinghams and then Nicholls Stores in the 1950's. There was another grocer's called Wheelers which became the Central Stores and is now Agora. The Nicholls family also ran the Agora premises as a grocery shop. In 1916, Frederick Sears was a family grocer, provision merchant and market gardener. In 1921 there was a shop called C. Griffin – tea and coffee warehouse, grocery and provisions.

There was a boot and shoe industry in Wendover for about two hundred years. In 1916 there was a bootmaker and repairer in the High Street called O.Beeson. The premises between the Forge and Woolerton House has been a shoe shop for a very long time firstly as Ivatts, then Barbara Charles and is now Well-heeled of Wendover. Next door number 3 High Street was a saddler's shop owned by Mr. R. White with a blacksmith's forge behind. In 1919 it became GHC Daniels, newsagent, bookseller and stationer. It was later Bracks and then Forbuoys and is now The Forge Boutique. In the 1960's and 1970's there was a newsagent called Godwins at the top of the High Street.

Number 1 High Street became a hardware store called Hampshire's and then John's Hardware before trading in luxury goods as Number One. The gentlemen's outfitters at Freemans became a television repair shop and then an extremely useful Aladdin's Cave of household goods run by Mr. and Mrs. J. Elliott.

What is now Christopher Pallet and a barber's shop next door was, at the beginning of the 1900's the premises of the watchmaking and jewellery business of Ernest J. Sharp who advertised his trade with a giant Ingersoll pocket watch hanging outside. He also ran a cycle department. There was later a jeweller called Stocks and after the Second World War there was Hamilton's, a jeweller in what is now 'Shu-shu'. There was a chemist's shop called Woodward's. By the end of the century most of the traditional family run shops had disappeared but we now have a selection of modern shops which still attract people to our High Street.

Early in the twentieth century a stage coach used to run to and from London stopping to pick up Wendover passengers outside 'The Red Lion' despite the fact that there had been a direct rail service to London for many years. After four hundred years 'The Red Lion' continues to serve the needs of local people and travellers. It did at one time have an off licence but now concentrates on being a restaurant and hotel and has recently undergone a thorough refurbishment.

'The King's Head', with a brewery owned by J.S. Holland Junior behind it, was still a lively part of the Wendover scene. By 1936 the brewery had closed but the public house continued until 1960. Mrs Knight the landlady ran it as a Free House which proved an advantage during the Second World War when beer was scarce. Mrs. Knight and her daughter Yvonne travelled around the neighbourhood purchasing beer from Chesham, Tring and Aylesbury to keep their customers happy. Behind the pub were five acres of gardens, a large orchard and outbuildings including an oast house. One had a large fireplace which had been used by the maltsters and brewers and their tools for shovelling hops hung on the wall. In the 1930's the CTC (The Cyclist's Touring Club) advertised the inn to their members who came and slept in the largest of the outbuildings. There were also gardens and fields behind 'The Red Lion'. Brackleys Path ran from the High Street between the greengrocer's shop and the apple orchard. There was a kissing gate at the end of this path which then turned diagonally across to the Heron Path and Witchell Meadow where there were several ponds. All of this disappeared when the public house was demolished in May 1965 to build the King's Head Parade, the public library and the car park. There were five shops, a butcher, William Crompton's furniture store, Sketchley's, a building society and a greengrocer. The ponds were drained in order to build the houses of Witchell.

On the opposite side of the High Street where they had stood since Tudor times were 'The Two Brewers' and 'The Swan'. In the 1980's they became 'The Swan and Brewers' and a restaurant called Rossini's. From the spring water in ancient times through the inns built on the Icknield Way to the present day, visitors to Wendover have always been able to find refreshment. As well as the inns and public houses there have been a number of cafés and tearooms. In the High Street alone there were Churchills' Café, The Wenda Café and the Friar Tuck. Currently, we have Crumbs, the Chocolaterie and Indulgence as well as the excellent Chinese Peking Restaurant.

As well as shops and eating places there have been many businesses originally associated with the local farming industry but later adapting to life in the twentieth century. At the turn of the century Vine Tree Farm in Back Street was still operating as a farm kept by John Field Archer and then by Joseph Holland, father of Joseph Senior Holland. Farming hit hard times in the 1930's as a result of the Depression and Vine Tree Farmhouse was left empty and the land taken on by the Spittles family of Manor Farm. It was then bought by the Hibberd family who ran a garage and motor repair shop on the land behind the farmhouse. This was demolished in the 1960's and the land sold by Mr. Parsons to Buckinghamshire County Council who built bungalows for senior citizens whose address is Vinetrees. A row of modern shops has been built on the farmyard facing Back Street. The cottages further up Back Street between Pear Tree Cottage and Freeman's were demolished to build more bungalows in Holland Close.

The Manor Waste has seen many changes in the last one hundred years. From early times it was the venue for the two agricultural fairs in May and October. These occupied the Manor Waste, Pound Street, London Road and part of Dobbins Lane. Even until the early 1900's the May Fair saw the area full of animals being bought and sold. The area was unpaved and lit by gas lamps operated by the lamplighter Mr. George Blow. Carter's, established in 1812, was still a blacksmith's forge but in 1916 with his sons gone to war, Mr. Carter was forced to close down. The parish magazine reported 'the very oldest place of business in Wendover will no longer resound with the roar of the bellows and the ring of the hammer and anvil'. On their return in 1919 Ralph and Ronald Carter set up Carter's Garage, an enterprising venture as this was in the early days of motoring. They sold petrol and spares, ran a taxi service and hired out limousines. This too was demolished in the 1960's to make way for a supermarket called Bishop's. During the development evidence was found below ground of flooring and brickwork thought to be part of the monastery associated with Bosworth House, where during building work in the 1920's Mr. Frank Wood had discovered some 17th Century panelling. Beneath this were some fine wall paintings which are now in the Victoria and Albert Museum. From 1923 until 1983 the part of the building now occupied by Antiques of Wendover was the Post Office. Next to Bosworth House was the coach building and wheelwright's premises of Joseph Floyd. The two gardens of Bosworth and Mr. Floyd's house joined and the part now known as Floyd's Yard was an orchard. All the ironwork for Mr. Floyd's business was done by Mr. Carter until 1901 when he decided to build his own forge and the road between the two properties now leads to Floyd's Yard. With the gradual demise of horse-drawn wagons in favour of motorised transport Joseph Floyd used his coach building skills to advantage, still doing fine woodwork and paint finishes, making canvas hoods and celluloid windows for the cars of the 1920's. He also made coffins and was in demand for sign writing and the painting of inn signs. The forge was used by Freddie Birch who, despite being only five feet tall, had a way with the shire horses being shod. Floyd's continued into the 1930's and the Depression but in 1938 they were forced to call it a day. Freddie Birch continued his trade for some years, dying at a ripe old age in the 1970's.

Harry Wood, brother of Frank, had his own business in the High Street as a builder and contractor (to HM War Office in 1915) in the premises once known as Tratt's Corner, which is now the home of Wendover Bookshop.

A new addition to the High Street in 1920 was the National Provincial Bank, designed by local architect Ernest George Theakston. After a period as a National Westminster Bank and briefly a gymnasium it is now the very popular Rumsey's Chocolaterie which brings a continental air to the Manor Waste.

Wendover has long had a charter which 'granted the right of the Citizens and Burgesses of Wendover that a fair be holden on two feast days'. The cattle fairs became fun fairs, the showmen coming every May and October to preserve this right. The large and brightly polished traction engines provided power and lighting. There was a large roundabout with its magnificent, brightly painted horses all with names painted on the neck, swingboats, coconut shies, roll the ball, hook-a-duck, a penny arcade, toffee apples and candy floss. This picturesque scene and the brightly painted Romany caravans parked up Dobbins Lane have disappeared since the 1960's but the charter still applies and is maintained by Mr. Pettigrove who brings his roundabout twice a year.

In 1877 the old stocks and lock-up or cage were moved from the Clock Tower to the Manor Waste where the War Memorial now stands and was known for years as Cage Bank. This site was used on many civic occasions, such as the return of the local Buckinghamshire Yeoman from the Boer War when, after arriving on the fire engine, they and the welcoming crowds were addressed by the vicar. Wendover's memorial to those who died during the 1914-18 War was erected here and in later years it was enclosed in an area of garden. After the Second World War the names of those who had given their lives were added to the memorial. Every year on Remembrance Sunday in November wreaths are laid by the British Legion and others before processing to St. Mary's Church.

When Bishop's supermarket (later Budgen's) was built in the 1960's the area in front was used as a car park until the library car park was finished. Until 1976 it still belonged to the Lord of the Manor, Lionel Abel-Smith, but he paid for it to be renovated and repaired to celebrate the Queen's Silver Jubilee in 1977 and it is now owned and administered by Wendover Parish Council on behalf of the village. In 1983, after almost one hundred years, the weekly market was revived and now takes place every Thursday. The celebrations for the Millennium in 2000 and the Queen's Golden Jubilee in 2002 were centred on the Manor Waste.

Until the early twentieth century Dobbins Lane was a narrow cart track, with hedges and tall trees on each side between open fields, once known as Dame Agnes Lane. It led to Cold Comfort Farm whose 17th century farmhouse was restored by Theakston in the 1920's. Cows were driven from their pastures along Dobbins Lane to be milked at Vine Tree Farm and Lime Tree Farm. A footpath cut across the land from the railway station and entered Windmill Meadow, then known as Adam's Meadow, near the top of the tennis courts and went straight across the meadow to Mill Path. The How family had a chicken farm where the tennis courts and bowling green are now until 1952. One could see the Aylesbury Road from Dobbins Lane until the 1970's.

In 1900 some residential development had started at the far end of the lane and the Mission Church of St. Agnes was built in 1909. Between the wars further building took place along the middle section of the lane and along its side roads of Perry Street and Chiltern Road and the road was widened in consequence. Dr. Rose the GP lived there keeping his horse and carriage in an old coach house next door. He always kept a dish of sweets in his hallway for his younger patients. Being spacious with large gardens, some houses were used as private schools namely Lady Margaret School and Coniston House. In 1950 one property became The Vicarage when the Reverend Pratt and his wife moved from Winterton House. What is now the houses of Vicarage Close was its garden! Gradually what was left of the fields has been built on. Thornton Crescent, Millmead and Vinetrees were all developed from the 1950's onwards and a number of individual properties in between. St. Agnes' Church was removed in 1990 and 51 Dobbins Lane built in its place. In 2001 a brand new vicarage was built next door to the old one which is now privately owned. However, on occasion Mr. Mogford can still be seen with his faithful sheepdogs moving sheep from the fields beyond Lionel Avenue along Dobbins Lane to pasture south of the village.

On the corner of Dobbins Lane and the Manor Waste there was a dairy run by Mr. Saunders and on the opposite corner of Pound Street stood a grocer's shop once Blake's, then Kinghams, followed by Seago's then Nicholls which is now Thresher's Off Licence. In the early 1900's Mr Blake ran it as a grocer's shop but also as an outfitters, hardware store and furnisher's upstairs. There were warehouses at the back and the outside of the shop was often adorned with frying pans and other goods. Many of the shops sold a variety of merchandise in those days. Mr Kingham's shop had tins of loose biscuits with glass tops, drawers and metal containers of cereals and spices, teas and coffees, dried fruit and sacks of sugar weighed out into blue paper bags. The butter was patted into shape for the customers and rounds of cheeses were wire-cut to within a half-ounce of their desired weight.

Mr Kingham also sold clothes and furniture before becoming a wholesaler. Seago's was followed by Nicholls Stores in 1946. The family had run a shop in Aston Clinton. Mr. and Mrs. Nicholls, their two sons and a daughter ran a high class grocers serving ten different prime ministers at Chequers including Winston Churchill. The Barlow family at Boswells were regular customers, as was the Toc H organisation in Forest Close which provided bed and breakfast for the visiting families of apprentices at RAF Halton. The Nicholls family also ran the first self-service grocery shop in the area at 12a High Street (now Agora) until 1988 and Peter Nicholls kept the Pound Street shop going until his retirement in 1994.

Thompson's bakery, next door to Nicholls', was in business until 1953, still delivering to outlying districts by pony trap. It became Balls' bakery and then The Anne Boleyn bakery before opening as a restaurant called Le Bistro. Further up, beside Lime Tree House, there was in the 1930's a Model Laundry which had moved from the Aylesbury Road. 21 Pound Street was Goodson's butchers shop. The oldest business in Pound Street is 'The Shoulder of Mutton'. In 1900 the landlord Fred Pedel was also the agent for the Great Central and Metropolitan Railway as well as a parish councillor. The inn was renamed 'The Railway Hotel' and visitors to the town were accommodated and beer consumed whilst waiting for trains. Mr Pedel encouraged use of the land behind the hotel for pub games such as quoits. There were even competitive quoits matches including an annual match with a team from 'The King and Queen'. In 1903 the grassy area was converted into a three-rink bowls green which became the Wendover and Chiltern Hill Bowls Club. In the 1930's they had a wooden club house which was used for the club's annual dinner and occasionally for entertainments and parties for children. During World War Two it was the headquarters of the Wendover Home Guard but sadly it was later destroyed in a fire. In 1951 the club bought its site in Dobbins Lane where they played for the first time in 1954. There is a centenary booklet in the Public Library which tells the full story. Also in 1951 'The Railway Hotel' reverted to its original name 'The Shoulder of Mutton'.

The railway station was an extremely busy place at the start of the 20th century having a spacious goods yard and signal box as well as passenger traffic. Marylebone Station was opened in 1899 and express trains came through Wendover on their way to Leicester and Sheffield. During the 1914-1918 war a one and three quarter mile branch line was built. The Puffing Billy locomotive transported coal to Halton House and returned with timber from Wendover Woods. There was still a timberyard in the 1930's. In Forest Close there had been a cinema but from 1916 through to the 1930's this was the site of the Hippodrome Theatre owned by Mrs. Marshall. There was a different programme every night, front seats cost 9d or one shilling and seats in the gallery only 3d, and it was very popular with soldiers from the camp. Between the wars, Wendover was one of the most popular destinations for Londoners with cheap day tickets for ramblers. The station was also used by RAF apprentices arriving for their entrance examination. When going on leave, they marched to catch special trains at 6am headed by a pipe band. There were steam engines through here until 1966. We have lost the express trains which went as far as Manchester but we still have a through route to Marylebone on Chiltern Railways which is one of the best in the country.

Beyond the railway past Bacombe Terrace a number of large houses have been built along the Ellesborough Road. Coombe Cottage was built by Theakston in 1914 for his sisters and he lived there himself in the 1940's. The cottages on the south side of Pound Street now belong to the Wendover Community Trust. This was set up in 1977 to receive the rents of these and other buildings, the proceeds of which to be used to benefit the people of Wendover. One cottage bears a plaque which reads 'This house and others in this street were given to the Wendover Community Trust by the Lord of the Manor, Lionel Abel-Smith Esq. to commemorate the Silver Jubilee of Her Majesty Queen Elizabeth II in 1977.' On the corner of Pound Street and South Street (London Road) there were two more cottages and a cake and sweet shop run my Miss Nora Thorne, sister of Arnold the barber in Aylesbury Street. Miss Thorne was very kind to all children however much or little they had to spend. All three of these properties were demolished in order to widen the road when traffic through the village increased.

Next door Bert Landon's newsagent shop and printing works survived. He had two small hand fed treadle presses and a flatbed poster press all crammed into a small space but he managed to supply the neighbourhood with posters, although not always correctly spelt. He also presented cinema shows in the Public Hall. His premises later became the Landon Tearooms which are now called Le Petit Café. In the 1930's the Mission Hall next to this was run by Miss Baldwin as a kindergarten during the week and used as a religious meeting place on Sundays. After the Second World War it became home to the Roman Catholic Church in Wendover. Of the three wattle and daub cottages along South Street dating from 1620 two were demolished in the 1960's and replaced with a property built in old brick. The remaining cottage is now Grade II listed and has been beautifully restored in keeping with its heritage.

On the other side of South Street in the early 1900's stood a rope and sack business run by Albert Payne. There had been a rope making industry for many years but Abel Rance was the last spinner and the spinning shed was now used by Mr. G. Brackley as a fowl shed. Number 1, South Street was the Post Office from 1915 until 1923 and Dean's Stores, a general provisions shop which sold food and all sorts of useful things. Further along the road a house now painted white was the home of Dr Hamilton in the 1920's and 30's and the bungalow with a horse's head on the end was Mrs. Franklin's Lilac Tea Café. Past 'The King and Queen' public house there were open fields where the giant steam engines of Pettigrove's Fair stood until allowed onto the High Street for the fairs in May and October. In the 1930's the whole of Witchell was still open fields with a gushing stream flowing into the millstream. The Witchell ponds were less deep than Hampden Pond so, in winter when they froze over, which was common then, the children skated and played ice hockey. In spring and summer they fished in the stream. Cows grazed on Witchell Meadow but it is now used by Wendover Cricket Club.

14

New Neighbours

1901 to the Present Day

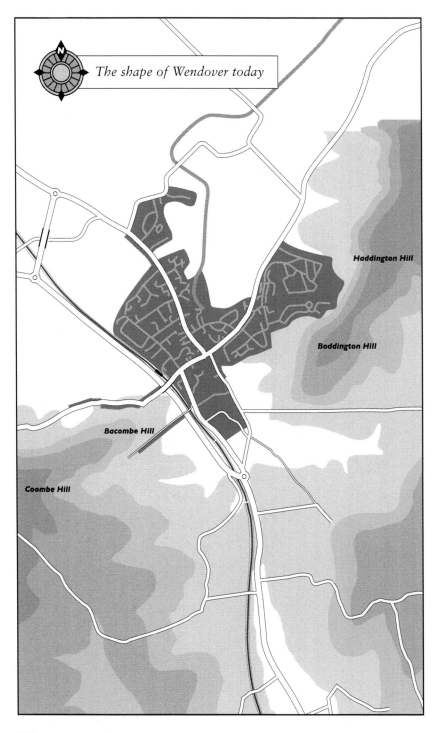

The shape of Wendover today

Haddington Hill

Boddington Hill

Bacombe Hill

Coombe Hill

Aylesbury Street, known originally as North Street, from the crossroads to the Manor Farmhouse and The Grange, had been an important part of the Borough since the 1500s. Beyond were farmers' fields and water meadows until, due to the building of the railway in 1892, the town expanded. Throughout the twentieth century houses were being erected along the length of the road to Aylesbury and to each side as far as the limit of the parish at Worlds End.

After the National School had moved to the new premises in 1869 the old coaching inn on the corner of Back Street and Aylesbury Street had several functions. Until well into the 1900s it still provided accommodation for the schoolmaster and to the right of the carriage arch on the ground floor was the Parish Room. Here on quarter days the agent of the Lord of the Manor collected the rents due on his large number of properties in the parish. There was by now a parish council but the Vestry still met in the Parish Room. The Vestry now consisted of the Vicar and 'all persons who pay rates or occupy premises that are rated for the relief of the poor in respect of the parish'. In Holy Week, Maundy money was issued here. Until the 1950s the Corner House was run as a hotel originally under the management of Mr. W. Pullein. Before the carriage arch was filled in there were porters stairs at the back up to the bedrooms. There was a billiards room, a card room and through the doorway with the lantern overhead was the Labourers' Club room where dances were held frequently. Behind the hotel were the Corner House Tea Gardens with a separate entrance from Back Street. It was later run by Miss Baddeley and Miss Curwen and then Mrs. Armstrong. The Parish Room continued to be used for meetings of the Parochial Church Council, Mothers' Club and Women's Institute until the building was converted into apartments.

Next door there had been a small grocer's shop run by Mr. Pearce, forerunner to a larger shop in the High Street. This was now the premises of a barber's shop run by a Mr. F.J.Thorne and his son Arnold. There was always much discussion between Arnold and his customers so there was no use in being in a hurry. He was also a fireman so it was not unknown for a client to be left with half a haircut if Arnold was called away during his turn. Between numbers 7 and 9 Aylesbury Street stood the fire station with two large foldback doors built in 1877. The voluntary firemen were summoned from their main occupations by the bell in the Clock Tower originally and later by a hooter. The horses were stabled at Bucksbridge Farm along the Heron Path and when the alarm sounded Edgar Saunders harnessed up the horses, two in good weather but three in bad and rode full tilt to the station. The volunteers stopped what they were doing instantly and on arrival donned their brass-buttoned uniforms and shiny helmets. The engine was still horsedrawn until 1928 when the first motorised fire engine was bought, again by public subscription. The fire station was in use until the 1960s when a modern headquarters was built further down the Aylesbury Road. In its place stand two cottages named King's Folly and Fyre.

Behind the next row of properties stood the yard of Frank Wood who advertised in 1915 as "Builder, Contractor, Undertaker and General Household Decorator", with a shed for the manufacture of coffins. The business continued for many years but this area is now occupied by flats known as Woods Place. Where we now have The Raj Indian Restaurant, there was once a grocer's shop called Keen's and in the 1960s E.G. and B.R. Knight. It later became an attractive gift shop with beams and low windows called Touch of Class. Beyond here was Manor Farm run by the Spittles family, its farmyard surrounded by a flint wall, behind which was Deering's Orchard and The Pennings. In the 1930s they took on Vine Tree Farm as well. Manor Farmhouse remains but after the Second World War, as farming declined, the land was sold for housing becoming Manor Road, Manor Crescent and Icknield Close. The John Colet School was built where their Great Barn stood and Wharf Road became a through road up to the Tring Road. The cottages between the Manor Farmhouse and The Grange remained on their island site until the 1970s when they were demolished to improve road access. There were three cottages, the closest to the Clock Tower being run as the Ivy Cottage Tearooms with a garden as well as accommodation available.

Before 1939 the small Roman Catholic community in Wendover worshipped at Halton but during the war St. Anne's convent and school in Ealing, London was evacuated to Bacombe Warren in Bacombe Lane and this became the place of worship for local Catholics. When the convent returned to Ealing fundraising began for a permanent church and St. Anne's Church on the Aylesbury Road opened in 1961. St. Anne's now shares its premises very successfully with the Wendover Free Church and is now known as Wendover Christian Centre. Both churches use it for their services and as the base for Churches Together in Wendover it is in constant use for all sorts of Christian activities.

The first 20th century housing built on Aylesbury Road was Chiltern Terrace built in 1910, some of which have been used as shops, including Fuller's the chemist which became Mary Dennis, hairdresser and another hairdresser's called Pearce's. At the northern end there was a butcher's shop with a tiny building behind used for slaughtering. In the 1930s it was Saunders, in the 1950s, J. Bolino and in the 1960s J. Wilde. It remained a butcher's shop until the 1980s when it became a Toc H charity shop for a while before being converted into a private dwelling. The land behind this terrace was known as Adams Meadow or Windmill Meadow until the houses on Millmead were built.

The windmill was in constant use during the 19th century and continued to operate into the 20th. Frank Purssell worked it from 1887 onwards assisted by Tobey Wood, who lived in the mill house, and Ernest Buggey. Frank built himself a new house facing the Aylesbury Road on what had been a filbert orchard. The steam engine installed in 1875 compensated for an inadequate supply of wind power but the situation was made worse by the building of houses along Aylesbury Road and Chiltern Road towards the end of the 19th century. After the sails were damaged by a storm in 1904, they were taken down and the mill was worked by steam only. Basil Purssell inherited the mill from his father in 1922 but by then cheap corn was being imported from abroad and he was buying imported grain from the London Docks and bringing it here by rail and road. However, it was the General Strike, which stopped supplies of coal for the steam engine, which caused the mill to close down in 1926 and it never worked again. The steam engine was broken up for scrap, the engine house and chimney were demolished.

In 1931 the tower mill was converted to a private residence and leased to Miss Marian Fawcett, a theatrical producer. In 1953 this was sold to Mr. and Mrs. Kenneth Roberton. Mr. Roberton was a musical publisher who from 1971 onwards ran his business from one of the upper floors, the parcels to be collected by the postman being lowered to ground level in a wicker basket on a pulley. On the ground floor members of a club gathered around the grand piano to enjoy guest musicians including the guitarist John Williams. The cap of the mill was replaced in 1969 and recently the whole building was completely refurbished and remains a private home.

On the corner of Chiltern Road stood a house called The Rosary which was converted in the middle of the 20th century to a Co-operative Society store run by Mr. Slade. There were three departments. In the grocery department at the front butter and cheese came in large blocks. Butter was weighed, patted with wooden paddles and a stamp put on top. Bacon was boned and sliced in the shop. The cashier sat in a glass booth. To the right was a butchery department and to the left a drapery department which sold sheets, towels, curtain material, haberdashery, knitting wool, underwear, jumpers and shoes. These were all stored in wooden drawers beneath glass-topped counters and Alice who served them knew where everything was.

Chiltern Road has Victorian, Edwardian, 1930s and 1960s housing. Along the next stretch of the Aylesbury Road are a number of late Victorian villas some of which have been used for shops and businesses. Number 93 was the house of the head gardener of the Rothschild Estate. Numbers 95 and 97 were occupied by the under gardeners. Behind them stood Wendover's first girl guide hut which in the 1950s became E. Crutchfield selling new and second-hand furniture. Numbers 101 and 103 were used as the police station, hence the name The Old Nick. Next door there was a building which has been a Salvation Army hall called The Barrack, a grocer's shop called Billington's, a pet suppliers shop called Greenpets and a motor spares shop. In 1916 it was a furniture and general stores run by Mr. C. Blake who made loose covers, curtains and blinds. J. Matthews, baker and confectioner, had his shop, with its bakery behind, which became Woodside's Bakery. On the corner of Perry Street, there was a World War One corrugated iron building which was run as a stationery business by Bert Landon until it became a small grocer's shop.

Vine Tree Farm once reached as far as Perry Street which is now a mixture of houses from late Victorian times onwards. The first houses were built by Mr. A. Perry Scivener, hence the name. Beyond here is a modern development on the site of Haglis House, once owned by the Purssell family, which was demolished in 1974. During the Second World War the house was used as a girls' home for evacuees. The current police station was opened in 1959. The first houses in Lionel Avenue date from the 1930s beyond which it was extended in the 1950s and 1960s over Cold Comfort Meadows as far as Dobbins Lane.

Just beyond Lionel Avenue there was a railway line from Wendover Station to Halton Camp with level crossing gates where it crossed the Aylesbury Road near the Ashbrook Recreation Ground. It was built to cope with the increased rail traffic during the 1914–1918 war. Coal and stock were transported to the Camp Power Station and timber brought down from Wendover Woods to be sent as pit props in the trenches. It was finally closed in 1963 and bungalows have been built each side of the road. The track alongside the allotments leads to Cold Comfort which for generations was a farm worker's home. In 1906 it was part of Castle Farm. The cottage stands on the bank of a stream which meanders through marshland but has since been enlarged and trees planted making it more secluded.

Before 1900 the east side of the Aylesbury Road was mostly damp meadowlands each side of the canal and the fields of Castle Park Farm, later owned by Basil Purssell and worked by Mr. Redding.

The top end of the parish was developed in the 1930s when Grenville Avenue, Carrington Crescent and Castle Park Road were created. In the 1940s there was a sawmill which made army huts, crates and boxes for the war. There was a dairy run by G and W. Crockett at 116 Aylesbury Road.

Ashbrook, which was given to Wendover by the Rothschild family, was the only recreation ground before the Second World War. In 1916 a large marquee was erected there to cater for soldiers and their visitors on Sunday afternoons. Bryants Acre was Wendover's football and cricket field. Wendover Football Club was particularly successful in the 1930s and their matches were well attended. In February 1921 the YMCA hut, which had been built in the school playground during the First World War as a leisure centre for the troops at Halton, was transferred to Bryants Acre to be used as Wendover Public Hall. It was a long, green hut with a stage and used in many different ways. During the Second World War, when evacuee children arrived here, it was partitioned by curtains into three extra classrooms but it was best known as The Sweat Box as it was heated by two old tortoise stoves which created a great deal of condensation. There were dances every Wednesday and Saturday, which were very popular with troops from Halton and guards from Chequers as well as the local young people, and this led to many romances between local girls and the RAF men. Basil Purssell provided the music on his piano and tea was brewed in a large samovar. To make the dance floor smoother bath salts were strewn over the floorboards. Extra people often moved in when the public houses closed and the police were often called. Fortunately, the police station was almost opposite The Sweat Box. There were also concerts to raise funds for causes such as Wings for Victory.

After the war there were annual parish parties at The Sweat Box. The entertainment was provided by local talent including Basil Purssell playing his drums. In 1951, when towns and villages all over the country held exhibitions to celebrate the Festival of Britain, ours was held there. When Wendover Memorial Hall was built in Manor Road, The Sweat Box became redundant and in the late 1960s, Bryants Acre was developed for housing.

The Red Rose garage has long been associated with transport. Its founder Bill Lancaster was a World War One pilot and he kept an aeroplane in a hangar from Halton rebuilt on the site. His mother ran a charity called Red Rose after which Bill named his aeroplane and when he went into partnership with the Hibberd family of Vine Tree House the name was adopted. The Red Rose Company set up the first bus service through Wendover in 1924. Between here and the Chiltern Ironworks a small corporation housing estate in the Garden Suburb style by local architect Ernest G. Theakston was built in 1920 just after the First World War. Hence the names Haig and Beatty cottages facing the Aylesbury Road and the cottages of Victory Road which replaced the lane between the canal and the windmill.

The Iron Works run by Edwin Caudrey became Gardener's motor garage with a single petrol pump. This was used as a factory during the Second World War. Between here and the Aylesbury Road a row of cottages had stood for many years, some of which became used as shops and a café. There was Digger (Harold) Caudrey's bicycle shop, Ted Deering's greengrocery premises, Mr. Eggleton's sweet shop and a cobblers called Oakleys, later run by Mr. Barnes. Right up to 1975 there was a wool shop supplying all the needs of the many people who still made their own clothes, but then the whole row were demolished as they were declared unsafe and in order to gain better access to the Health Centre.

In 1964 Gardener's garage had been replaced by a modern fire station in place of the small station in Aylesbury Street which had served its purpose well since 1877. The new station was manned by twelve volunteers until 1989, first summoned by a siren and then bells in their own homes. When the alarm sounded they downed tools and rushed to the fire station leaving the forecourt full of rapidly abandoned bicycles, cars and often a tractor. In 1973 the fire station was joined by a brand new health centre for Wendover. Dr. Colin Riley moved his surgery from The Red House and was joined by Dr. Tony Garrod, Dr. Brian Ballantine and Dr. Richard Leeper. Later the fire station was demolished and we are now served by Aylesbury Fire Station. The Health Centre was able to expand sideways when larger premises were required.

At the start of the twentieth century Wharf Road was just a dirt track with a flint wall on the corner, a couple of cottages and a huge gasometer. There was a coal and wood yard by the canal and a wooden crane used to unload the barges. Beyond the canal was a very large, marshy, gated field stretching to the Tring Road. By 1904 the canal leaked and its trade had been taken over by the railway so it was abandoned. The fields of Manor Farm became a housing estate in the 1950s. Until the 1960s Oliver's Stables stood on Wharf Road run by Mrs. Oliver, wife of Alan Oliver the showjumper. This too was built on in the 1970s and called The Paddocks.

The large houses between Wharf Road and the Clock Tower have been preserved by their owners and are all now private homes. Sturrick House remained as 'The Temperance Hotel' until the Second World War run by Mrs. North. Archway Cottage was the premises of a taxi and care hire business for a few years just after the war. The Red House was bought from the Lord of the Manor in the 1920s by Doctor Orme, a local GP for many years. The original consulting rooms were part of the house with an entrance under the carriage arch but Dr. Orme set up his surgery in a small building at the back. Dr. Colin Riley moved into The Red House in 1964 and used the surgery until 1973 when the Health Centre opened. The area of grass and trees outside The Red House still belonged to the Lord of the Manor. In 1965 Dr. Riley was surprised to see workmen with large saws draw up outside his home. When questioned he discovered they had been sent to fell the trees to make a car park. With help from Mr. Tony Mogford and other friends he was able to prevent this happening and this led to the formation of The Wendover Society to ensure the protection of the beauty and character of Wendover. The Society has done sterling work on behalf of the village ever since.

Several cottages, a thatched barn and gardens stood between The Red House and 'The George' until the 1920s when the area was redeveloped. Next to Lime Cottage was The Spinning Wheel Restaurant run by Miss Baddeley and Miss Curwen who had previously run The Corner House. The Spinning Wheel is now The Prince of India. New shop premises were built abutting

'The George' initially as a supplier of electrical goods run by Mr. and Mrs. S. White and their son Norman. It has since been Cyril Mitchell's electrical supplies and is now a hairdresser's. After 500 years as an inn 'The George' is still a successful hostelry, now called 'The George and Dragon'. When a tornado struck the area in 1950, giant hailstones damaged the top floor and the roof was rebuilt and in 1988 the building was completely refurbished. The building right on the corner of Aylesbury Street and Tring Road started life as four cottages but for many years now these have been used as shops. In the early years of the twentieth century it was a bread shop and bakehouse but by 1915 it had become R.J. Morgan selling tobacco, cigarettes, chocolates, stationery and fancy goods as well as bread. It was extremely popular with the soldiers from the camp at Halton during the war. R.J. Morgan also published a book called "Souvenir of Wendover" and became a printer and photographer. Between the wars the shop became G. Southern and Son, an attractive tobacconist and confectioner's and was extended to include the property that is now Julian's hairdressing salon, continuing trading for many years.

The tannery in Tring Road had ceased production in 1828 but when the Canal Company excavated this area in order to culvert the millstream, they discovered a great many bones. At Holly Cottage which stands on the site of St. John's Church, the chapel of ease many years ago, on levelling part of the garden, human bones were unearthed indicating its use as a burial ground at one time. At the start of the 20th century though, a Mr. Guntrip kept a vegetable garden on the land supplementing his income as a window cleaner by selling his vegetables. There is now a row of shops which were built in 1975. Until the Second World War Coldharbour Cottages were occupied by local families many of whom grew their own vegetables and some still kept pigs. In 1948 the new council houses were built opposite and many people moved from Coldharbour into these brand new houses. The cottages have become homes for private owners and now look very attractive with their white walls and well tended gardens.

A narrow entrance by 'The Packhorse' was the original access to the cottages of Clay Lane. Until 1910 a soup kitchen operated in

Prospect Place on Tuesdays, Thursdays and Saturdays, all paid for by Alfred de Rothschild. The poor were issued with cards to claim their soup and bread baked by local bakers, served by Jane White who had been a kitchen maid at Halton House. On the opposite corner to 'The Packhorse' there was a fish and chip shop and more cottages as far as the Congregational Church. After the Second World War the area of Clay Lane was redeveloped with the building of houses on The Poplars and in Clay Lane itself. The entrance was widened to accommodate motor traffic. The Congregational Church was rebuilt in 1903 on land donated by Mr. Allen Juson, a butcher who had once lived in Clay Lane. He also gave his private house next door and after he and his wife had both died it was used as the home of the minister of the church and called The Manse. Mr. Freeman of the department store in the High Street was a very active member of the Congregational Church and contributed generously to its rebuilding. There was great excitement when the daughter of Prime Minister Ramsay Macdonald was married there in the 1920s. The church was demolished in 1985 as the Free Churches in Wendover moved their services to the Christian Centre in Aylesbury Road. The homes built in its place are called Juson's Glebe.

At the start of the 20th century there were still cottages on the other side of the road called Bank Cottages, Bank Farm Cottages and Daisybank. At one end was The Chiltern Studio, owned by photographer Mr. Brooks who lived at The Manse. The old Tring Road continued on past the thirty cottages known as Casualty Row or York Buildings in front of more cottages and the Rose and Crown public house. After the new housing estate was built on the open fields to the south the road was widened. In the 1980s the third row of ten cottages was demolished in order to re-route the road to the left of 'The Rose and Crown'.

The fields on the slopes of Boddington Hill have become home to the residents of the houses built there in 1948, but we still have Bank Farm on the site of the farmhouse built in the 1400s. It is farmed by Mr. Tony Mogford and his son Edward. Dr. McConel who worked closely with Dr. Orme during the middle years of the century lived with his family at Paradise House. The area called Paradise is now known as Hale Road. A number of beautiful houses designed by Ernest Theakston were built on the eastern side of Hale Road in 1915. He built Garden House for himself as his home and studio. Marlowe House was called Up-Along when it was the home of the Holland family in the 1920s and 1930s. On the west side, Winterton House was occupied by the vicars of St. Mary's Church until the 1950s when it was converted and extended into a residential home for the elderly by Buckinghamshire County Council. Beyond that Bucksbridge Farm became a casualty of the decline in farming. In the 1960s and 1970s houses and bungalows were built on what had been fields. Hale Road leads to Hale Lane where several large houses were built during the first half of the twentieth century. In 1930 The House in the Field now called Mulberry Hill, was built for Sir Stanley Reed, a Conservative Party ally of Sir Bruce Hamilton. Ernest Theakston designed the end block with chauffeur's house a little later.

On the north side of Paradise House next to The Clock Tower stands Brook House, built in 1616, which has been home to a number of different families. With its seven bedrooms it was once a very grand house occupying a prominent position in the town. Until recently it was the home of Mr. Ian Kirk but sadly on 31st December 2007, it was seriously damaged by fire and is currently awaiting rebuilding. Fortunately, no-one was injured in the fire.

Since the time of the Domesday Book in 1086 a working watermill called the Nether Mill stood on the millstream behind what is now the site of the Old School. It continued working until 1931 under the ownership of Joseph Senior Holland, proprietor of 'The Red Lion'. Clad in white weatherboarding it can be seen amongst the trees behind the school. It was converted to a private residence by Captain Harry Slingsby who was the first man to land a plane at Halton airfield.

After the fire engine was removed to its purpose-built station in Aylesbury Street in 1877, the Clock Tower's main function for the next one hundred years was as a timekeeper. Until 1984 it was still laid out as a fire station with a fire engine bay, harness room and fuel bay.

At the back were the lockups and a men's urinal which had been bricked up when new conveniences were built in Back Street. The outside became used as a poster hoarding and creeper was allowed to grow and obliterate the lower part of the tower. Shortly after the Second World War, pigeons took to roosting in the tower which interfered with the workings of the clock and netting was installed to deter them. There was still a horse trough against the west wall.

In 1962 the building was officially presented to the Parish Council by Lionel Abel-Smith, great nephew of Philip Smith who had been responsible for the rebuilding project in 1870. At first the ground floor was used as a store for Parish Council property including the street cleaner's equipment. In 1984 John Yabsley, a local architect, redesigned the building to provide an information centre on the ground floor with accommodation for the Parish Clerk above.

The building was by then listed as a Grade II building of Special Architectural or Historic Interest by the Department of the Environment so alterations to the exterior were kept to a minimum. The old rough entrance doors were replaced by a handsome pair of glazed oak doors, a new window inserted into the blank arch facing the High Street and triangular windows inserted into the roof to light the upper floor. The lockup became a kitchen and toilet retaining the solid prison door. The work was carried out by William Ash Limited of The Lee and the reopening ceremony took place on 20th April 1985.

In 1992, using plans by Dr Ian Toplis, another local architect, the ground floor became a Tourist Information Centre with a new office above to meet the expanding duties of the Parish Clerk but no changes were made to the exterior. The original clock is still in use today. The Clock Tower at the focal point of the three main streets is now recognised as the symbol of Wendover.

The Literary Institute served the community well as a library and meeting place until the 1960's. Members of the Women's Institute ran a library service there on Thursdays for almost thirty years until the County Library opened in 1965.

The yard of The Red Lion today

The Two Brewers and The Swan

The Corner Shop and The George and Dragon (formerly The George Inn)

The site of the level crossing in Aylesbury Road

15

Slates to SATS

1901 to the Present Day

The village school then and now

The Headteacher of Wendover National School at the start of the 20th century was Mr John George Bushell and the Chairman of School Managers was the Reverend Albert Smith, vicar of St. Mary's Church, Lord of the Manor and chairman of Wendover Parish Council. Education was now free and the numbers of pupils attending school grew steadily to over three hundred in 1910. Mr. Bushell's successor was Mr Arthur W. Molineux. He brought many fresh ideas and the curriculum was expanded with more emphasis on creative pursuits, sports, domestic science and gardening. He established school gardens where boys and girls grew vegetables, fruit bushes and flowers. The children won many prizes at Wendover Flower Show. During World War I they grew vegetables to be sent to the navy.

The classrooms had high ceilings and windows and it was impossible for the children to see out. There was no separate hall for assemblies but folding doors between the classrooms were opened each morning for scripture lessons. The vicar or the curate came most days. Two very kind sisters, the Misses Burnett taught the infants for many years assisted by Miss Irvine. She wore long, black, swishy skirts and a boater with a very long feather and was rather severe. The classrooms were heated by coal fires and Miss Irvine liked to stand with her back to the fire discreetly lifting her hem at the back to warm her feet. On the first day at school the children were presented with their slates on which to work and paper cones filled with sweets. Among the teachers at the Mixed School were Mr Sear, Miss 'Tiger' Eldridge who played the piano, Miss Smith and Miss Jones. Lessons concentrated on reading, writing, grammar and mental arithmetic, much of it taught by parrot fashion chanting especially of times tables, but the results were good and the annual reports from HM Inspectorate were mostly full of praise. The older boys now learned woodwork and the girls were taught a variety of needlework including dress making. There was drill in the playground and netball.

Until 1932 the Mixed School and the Infant School were administered separately but in April that year they were amalgamated under the leadership of Mr. Percival William Jones. In 1934 the new headmaster was Mr. W.G.A. Morris who had a great interest in horticulture and during his time the gardens continued to flourish. He preserved the school traditions. On Empire Day the whole school assembled in the girls' playground to sing the National Anthem and salute the flag. On Ascension Day the children walked along the Heron Path to church with bunches of flowers which they laid in the churchyard. In 1936 the Hampden Meadow Recreation Ground was opened and the school now had a playing field near at hand. The football team became one of the best in the district.

In 1939 the headmaster was Mr. C.V. Burgess. There were 250 children aged from five to fourteen in eight classes. The school was very much part of village life. Each child was given fresh milk every day from Mr. Saunders' dairy in the High Street. A full school meals service began in 1939 but many children still went home for lunch. If children were injured at school they were taken by a teacher to the doctor along the road at the The Red House in Aylesbury Road. There were strong links with St. Mary's Church. But, as the children returned to school after the harvest holidays in 1939, with a war imminent they had to face many changes. What affected the children most was the influx of evacuees and their teachers from the London area. Having returned to school for only three days at the end of August, the school re-opened on the 19th September with over 130 extra children. At first Wendover children used the school building in the mornings and London children in the afternoons but by using the Public Hall in Aylesbury Road for extra classrooms, the school became a full time amalgamated school for 420 children and eleven teachers. As in the First World War the school gardens produced extra rations but in 1947 extra classrooms were built on this land beside the Heron Path.

Mr Burgess's successor in June 1948 was Mr. H.J. Figg Edgington later to become the Reverend Figg Edgington. His innovations included visits by pupils to the theatre and ballet as well as visits to the school by musical and theatrical groups. He introduced the school uniform of grey with a black and gold blazer and tie. He also instigated the Parent Teacher Association. In May 1951 new gates were installed at the school entrance 'in proud memory of old boys of Wendover School who gave their lives in two World Wars'. When the school moved to its current site, the Memorial Gates were removed to the new school driveway where they remain to this day. A Roll of Honour listing the names of those who died is displayed in Wendover C.E. Junior School.

The school was still very much at the centre of everyday life in the community but, due to the post war expansion of the town, the number on roll was to increase considerably from then on. By January 1953 there were over three hundred pupils in ten classes. There was by now a school hall but this was now needed as a classroom, the Parish Room across the road was used and when the school dentist came, the Literary Institute was hired for the purpose. By now central heating had been installed but in 1954, electricity was supplied for the first time. Various extensions were considered but the site was too small. As a result of this a new secondary school was opened in Wharf Road on 1st October 1956. It catered for 410 children aged from eleven to sixteen from Wendover, Halton, Weston Turville and other villages in the area. It was named The John Colet School after the man who was partly responsible for the first school in Wendover 450 years previously. The old school now took on Primary status. It became a Junior Mixed and Infants school with the age range of five to eleven years. In 1951 the school had been granted Voluntary Aided Status but this was now revoked and an order for Controlled Status issued. Although the Church retained ownership the School became controlled by the local Education Authority.

The worthy successor to the Reverend Figg Edgington in January 1965 was Mr. Ivor Pammenter who led the school through a period of great upheaval and change. The school continued as a place of opportunity in music, dance, sport and educational visits as well as a sound academic education. The first major change came with the opening of the new school for children aged five to seven years at the

Wharf Road site at Easter 1967. It was named the John Hampden School after Wendover's famous MP and Civil War hero. The new headmistress was Mrs G. Hatwell and she was joined by existing staff from the old school.

According to the Headmaster's Log Book, Wendover National School was established in January 1868. Therefore 1968 was celebrated as the school's centenary year with an exhibition, fair and pageant in June with children, parents and staff in Victorian dress.

In September 1973 the school became Wendover Church of England (Controlled) Middle School serving the 8+ to 12+ age range. It had been hoped originally that the change would coincide with the move to new premises in Wharf Road. The old school building, built by the Lord of the Manor Philip Smith in 1869 for the church and the village, served its purpose well for over one hundred years. Many thousands of children had passed through its doors, and it was a focal point for the whole community. However, Wendover had changed enormously in that time and now a change of location was needed. The school was auctioned and bought for £37,000 by a firm of property developers which converted it into five homes named after five of the headteachers during its history. Meanwhile school life carried on as usual but it must have been a strange and unsettling time for pupils and staff. At long last on the 9th October 1974, the children and staff took up occupation of their long awaited new school. Mr. Pammenter retired in 1992 after a long and successful headship passing the reins to Mr. K. G. Palmer who led the school into the 21st Century.

16

Faith and Fun

1901 to the Present Day

Faith and Fun

The Heron Path still follows the millstream from Witchell to St. Mary's Church. In 1909 school gardens were developed where girls and boys were given their own plot and taught how to make good use of it. The path, once lit by gas lamps, continues past the grounds of Winterton House and in front of Bucksbridge House and Heronpath House. This 1970's house was built on the site of the farmhouse and farmyard of Bucksbridge Farm which was farmed by the Saunders family who lived at Sluice Cottage. Edgar Saunders, son of George, continued to farm until after the Second World War when the farmland was used to build the houses and bungalows along Hale Road. Opposite Heronpath House is Rope Walk Meadow which has now been established as a wildflower meadow. The Heron Path continued via a stile past the sluice until it was diverted when Sluice Cottage was no longer part of a farm.

Hampden Meadow and Hampden Pond were used for farming by Charles Spittles until 1936 when they were passed to Wendover Parish Council as a new recreation ground. Until then there were just a few swings and a seesaw at Ashbrook in the Aylesbury Road. The meadow was donated by Sir Thomas Barlow of Boswells to celebrate the Silver Jubilee of King George V and Queen Mary. The playing equipment, shelter and toilets were of a very high order but sadly they became the target for vandals almost from the day the field was opened. The pond froze over most winters but was no longer used for skating as it had a history of claiming lives. In the 1930's Wendover Fishing Club had a boat and boat house there. It is now a popular area for recreation and is maintained by the Parish Council who issue permits for fishing.

St. Mary's Church now stands in a peaceful rural setting away from the traffic and bustle of the town. In 1900 the vicar was the Reverend Albert Smith who since 1894 had been the Lord of the Manor, on the death of his brother Philip, and first chairman of Wendover Parish Council. He was 'a tall man with a ginger-coloured beard and hair which was rapidly turning white who was a very strict but very kind-hearted man.' He retired in April 1914 having worked ceaselessly throughout his life to improve the lives of the people of Wendover. He made almost daily visits to the village school and on his death in August 1914 the Headmaster wrote in the school logbook 'on this day died the Reverend Albert Smith, until May last and for 47 years Vicar of Wendover. As vicar and for many years also correspondent to the school managers, no school ever had a kinder friend, more constant visitor or generous supporter. Teachers and scholars alike felt his loss when failing health compelled him to resign active duties, first as correspondent and then as vicar, but his death now makes us realise fully the greatness of our loss.' Albert's eldest son Major Edwin Philip Smith succeeded his father as Lord of the Manor and came to live at Bucksbridge House. On his death in 1936 the position was bequeathed to his brother Brigadier General Lionel Abel Smith whose eldest son, also named Lionel has been our Lord of the Manor since 1946, when he was only twenty two years old and studying law in London. He has continued his family's tradition of devoted service to the people of Wendover.

In 1914 there was cause for concern over the dangerous condition of the church tower. G.H. Fellowes Prynne was employed to rescue it which he did by means of a discreet steel frame inserted into the structure, a rebuild of the north side and refacing of the rest of it. A new heating system with an enlarged boiler room was installed, the clock was repaired, the five bells recast and a new bell added dedicated to Albert Smith who died in August 1914. After the First World War the churchyard was extended across the ground where the coach road to the old vicarage had been. When the first graves in this new area were dug several human skeletons were found. There is nothing in the church records about burials here so the area must have been a burial ground long before the church records began in 1670.

In 1929 the south chancel aisle was converted to a Lady Chapel in memory of Reverend T.W. Hudson who had been vicar for eight years.

Heron Path

St Mary's Church

Oak panelling, a new altar, an ambry and seating were added in the low-key Gothic church style of the inter-war period. The architect was Austin Durst who lived at The Grange in Aylesbury Street and the work carried out by H. Wood of Wendover. In 1955 the interior of the whole church was brightened with a coat of limewash. In the 1960's the central Sunday service became the Parish Eucharist during which the priest, standing with his back to the congregation at the extreme east end of the church was still a somewhat remote figure. Early in the 1980's the church was again rearranged to suit the changing pattern of worship. The organ and choir were restored to their original position at the west end of the nave. The Communion Table was positioned under the chancel arch giving a much closer involvement between the priest and the congregation. The clergy vestry moved to the south porch and the space released in the north chancel aisle became the St. Mary's Centre. A new floor divided it into a meeting room on the upper floor over a smaller room, kitchen and toilets on the ground floor creating a meeting place for the whole community.

Until 1921, the Churchwardens were the only official representatives of the laity in each parish and had considerable local status. Parochial Church Councils were then established in the Church of England and now carry much of the responsibility for all aspects of church life and the duties of churchwardens have changed. In those days Sundays were quiet and observed days when almost everyone went to church. The walks to and from church were quite a ritual and in the 1920's to be in the choir at St Mary's was the 'in thing'. At first one had to serve as a probationer sitting behind the choir stalls near the organist. The organ bellows had to be pumped by whoever was available. It was a proud moment when a choirboy was promoted to the main choir. The services were Matins and Evensong on Sundays, Evensong on Wednesdays and choir practice on Fridays for which each choirboy received four pence a week.

Funerals were often very solemn occasions with a slow procession up the High Street and along the London Road, headed by a walking escort in formal funeral attire with tall black hats. On Armistice Day, the 11th November, there was a procession past the war memorial led by the full RAF band from Halton to the tightly packed church. The Second World War brought about a change in church attendance and attitudes. The evening service during the winters of the war was at three o'clock to avoid the hours of the blackout and was held in dim candle light and a few muted lamps.

The Parish Church has been at the centre of community life for over seven hundred years. In June 1990 the church celebrated its 700th anniversary with a service of thanksgiving. The survival of this beautiful historic building depends entirely on the people of Wendover, which is why the Friends of St. Mary's was formed in 1994 as a non-religious, non-sectarian body. Nearly £200,000 has been raised to be spent exclusively on the fabric of the building and more will be needed in the future to preserve Wendover's oldest building for future generations. However, the focus of Wendover's everyday life has long since moved to the High Street leaving the church building remote from the town. In order to fulfil their vision of 'a church at the heart of the community' the members of St. Mary's Church have started by establishing the @ St. Mary's shop at 11 High Street, following in the footsteps of the Mediaeval farmers. It serves as a contact point for churchgoers and non-churchgoers alike as well as an administrative centre for all the churches in Wendover.

More details of the full history of St. Mary's Church can be found in booklets available in the church which is now open daily. During the summer months teas are served on Sunday afternoons.

Being one of the highest points of the escarpment, Coombe Hill, with its monument, is a landmark for miles around. Old photographs show that it was clear of trees due to grazing, and the woodland growth happened during the twentieth century. The Monument, erected to the memory of 148 men of Buckinghamshire who fell in the Boer War (1899–1902) in South Africa, was unveiled on 4th November 1904. This was marked by a procession, including a band, from the Clock Tower to the top of the hill for a ceremony followed by a bonfire.

The summit of Coombe Hill had long been a tourist attraction and access to the Monument was by a footpath leading from Wendover. In 1906 Sir John Lawson Walton, Attorney General at that time, built Coombe Hill House on land he had bought from Lord Rothschild. He then had fences erected across the footpath which had been used by the public for years. Although stiles had been put into the fences the inhabitants of Wendover were incensed and a letter was sent from the Parish Council demanding their removal within seven days. When this failed to happen the towncrier announced that a visit would be made to destroy the stiles. On the evening of 21st June 1906 an estimated two thousand people climbed the hill to witness the removal of the stiles as the crowd sang the National Anthem. The dispute continued for another six months until Sir John had kissing gates installed instead and the right to roam at will remains to this day.

Since 1918 Coombe Hill has been owned by the National Trust. In 1938 the Monument was almost completely destroyed by lightning and was rebuilt by Buckinghamshire County Council, after which it was camouflaged throughout the Second World War to prevent its use as a landmark by enemy aircraft.

Despite two wars and the Depression the people still managed to enjoy themselves. The coronations of King Edward VII, King George V, King George VI and Queen Elizabeth II have all been celebrated with church services, processions and parties. The Silver Jubilee of King George V and Queen Mary in 1935 was celebrated with a parade of floats and sports on Bryants Acre. The Silver Jubilee and Golden Jubilee of Queen Elizabeth and the Millennium in 2000 have all been times of celebration for the whole community.

In 1951, to coincide with the Festival of Britain, Wendover Parish Council put on an exhibition in the village hall (at that time this was the former YMCA hut situated at Bryants Acre). Councillor Harry Bates JP, Chairman of the Parish Council for many years, who took a great interest in the history of Wendover, made a series of wall charts. In 1971 Wendover won the De Fraine Cup for the best kept village with a population of over one thousand in Buckinghamshire.

To celebrate there was an exhibition in the County Library organised by the library staff out of which came the book 'The New History of Wendover'. This included prints of Harry Bates' wallcharts and the whole of 'The History of Wendover' by Sir Leonard West.

For many years during the 1970s and 80s there was an annual carnival in the grounds of Wendover House School. This would feature a funfair, Miss Wendover competition, children's fancy dress competition, dog show, art show, morris dancing, gymnastic displays by RAF apprentices and other attractions. The proceeds were used to build the swimming pool at the John Colet School for use by the whole community. There have always been a great many different clubs and societies in Wendover whose members contribute greatly to these community events. The influx of newcomers has added to the richness of our heritage.

Two thousand years ago a small group of people chose to make their homes here because of good fresh water and abundant resources to grow food and build homes. I think that they made a wise choice. Wendover is a good place to live. We still have the unspoilt hills and the stream of bright water which attracted the early settlers in the first place. Eight hundred years on we still have our parish church, the only building to survive from those early days and now part of a wider Christian family in Churches Together in Wendover. Much of the beauty of the church and the picturesque appearance of the town we owe to the Smith family. After all these years we still have a Lord of the Manor, Lionel Abel Smith Esq., who cares about this place and its people. We certainly owe a great deal to the Smith family, our Lords of the Manor for over two hundred years.

In 1969 parts of the village were designated as a Conservation Area and the Wendover Society has worked hard to preserve its unique character. Now home to about eight thousand inhabitants we have come a long way since the time of the Domesday Book but Wendover is still a very special place. Long live Wendover!

Origin of Street Names

Addington Cottages	*John Hiley Addington MP 1796-1802*
Ashbrook	*Ancient piece of watermeadow*
Back Street	*The original main street which became a back street when Fore Street evolved.*
Bacombe Terrace	*Cottages on lower slopes of Bacombe Hill*
Barlow Road	*Sir Thomas Barlow, doctor to Queen Victoria*
Birdcage Walk	*Path to scrubwood*
Bryants Acre	*Ancient name for farmland*
Burke Road	*Edmond Burke MP 1765-1773*
Canning Road	*George Canning MP 1796-1801*
Carrington Crescent	*Robert Smith, Lord Carrington, friend and adviser of Pitt*
Cavendish Close	*Richard Cavendish MP 1761-1764*
Chandos Place	*Marquis of Chandos*
Chesham Road	*Old name for Hale Road*
Clay Lane	*The Clays, large area of farmland*
Colet Road	*John Colet, Dean of St. Paul's Cathedral*
Compton Road	*Miss Compton of the Hale who endowed the Memorial Hall*
Dame Agnes Lane	*Original name of Dobbins Lane*
Dark Lane	*Footpath between Heron Path and Hale Road*
Drunken Green	*The crossroads of Church Lane and Hale Road*
Drunken Man Lane	*The Hale – where drunks from 'The Wellhead' inn might end up if lost*
Grenville Avenue	*Sir Richard Grenville MP 1714-1720*
Haglis Drive	*Built on site of Haglis House*
Hampden Road	*John Hampden MP 1623-1643, hero of the Civil War*
Hazeldene	*Houses on site of Hazeldene House*
Holland Close	*J. Holland, mayor of Aylesbury*
Icknield Close	*Houses close to route of Icknield Way*

Juson's Glebe	*Houses on land donated by Juson to the Congregational Church*
King's Head Parade	*Shops on site of 'The King's Head' inn*
Liffre Drive	*Wendover is 'twinned' with Liffre in France*
Lime Tree House	*Farmhouse of Lime Tree Farm*
Lionel Avenue	*Houses on land owned once by Lionel de Rothschild. We have also had two Lords of the Manor named Lionel Abel Smith*
Manor Road	*Houses built on Manor Farm*
Millmead	*Houses on land close to the windmill*
The Paddocks	*Houses on the land of Oliver's Stables*
Paradise Lane	*Old name for Hale Road*
Perry Street	*A. Perry Scrivener – builder*
The Poplars	*Land behind The Grange on old maps*
Reddings Close	*A tenant farmer called Mr. Redding*
St. Agnes Gate	*Small church in Dobbins Lane*
Spiteful Corner	*Area of grass near 'The Wellhead' inn where fights often took place*
Stanhope Close	*Philip Henry Stanhope MP 1806-1807*
Thornton Crescent	*Rev. Spencer Thornton, Vicar of Wendover 1837-1850*
Vicarage Close	*Houses built on garden of vicarage in Dobbins Lane*
Victory Road	*Named just after World War One*
Vinetrees	*Bungalows built on land of Vine Tree Farm*
Walnut Way	*Overlooks Walnut Meadow*
Watermeadow Way	*Built on area of watermeadows*
Woollerton Cresent	*Dr. Edwin Goodburn Woollerton, GP*

Acknowledgements

This history could not have been written without my first reading the following books. I would like to thank all the authors for laying the foundations of what has been an interesting and enjoyable voyage of discovery about the place in which I live.

'The Book of Wendover'
by Max Summerell, Brian Samuels, Alan Mead and Peter Eckett
A detailed historical account of Wendover, including geological and political facts.

'The New History of Wendover 1972'
edited by Richard Snow
A book based on an exhibition in Wendover library.

'The History of Wendover'
by Leonard H. West
Written early in the 20th century, a great resource of information about the political life of Wendover in the context of history.

'A Tour of Wendover with Scraps of History'
by J. Stoddart Cox

'Wendover'
by Elizabeth Cull
A small well-written book giving the essence of Wendover.

'Wendover in old picture postcards'
by Colin J. Seabright
A collection of 76 images of the area.

Acknowledgements

'Around Wendover and Halton'
by Paul Dabrowski and John How
A pictorial tour of Wendover.

'Wheelwrights, Watering Cans and Witchell'
A fascinating account by four members of the Floyd family, covering the first half of the twentieth century.

The illustration of the Market House *(p23)* and the Dame Mary Wolley map *(p30)* were kindly loaned by Mr. Lionel Abel-Smith. The illustration of the village school *(p130 top)* was drawn by the late Mr Basil Purssell and was kindly loaned by Wendover C of E Junior School.

I have also had the privilege and pleasure of talking to a number of people who have shared their own personal recollections of life in Wendover during the twentieth century. Wendover comes across as a happy place to live. Life was hard at times and people have had to work very hard, but there was a lot of fun, too. I wish to thank particularly, Mr. Lionel Abel-Smith, Mrs. Olive Beecham and her sister, Mrs. Mollie Brett, the late Mr. Henry Buggey, Mrs. Pat Cooper, the late Mr. William Crompton, Mrs. Yvonne Butler, Mrs. Marion Lodge, Mrs. Peggy Mitchell, Mrs. Val Moir, Mrs. Peggy Newman, the late Mr. Peter Nicholls, the late Mr. Ron Philbey, Dr. Colin Riley and the late Dr. Ian Toplis.

I would also like to thank friends, too numerous to mention, who have been a constant source of encouragement and useful suggestions and the people who have helped me to prepare my work for publication. They are, Mrs. Barbara Eccleston, Mr. Daniel Gosling, Mrs. Pauline Greasby, Mr. Dennis Harrison, Mrs. Barbara Jefford and the late Mr. Bernard Roberts.

But most of all I would like to thank my husband Ian Gosling for his constant love and support.